WILL TO SURVIVE

Other Books By
Jane Middelton-Moz

After The Tears with Lorie Dwinell

Shame And Guilt

Children of Trauma

Also Available on Audiocassette

WILL TO SURVIVE

Affirming The Positive Power Of The Human Spirit

Jane Middelton-Moz, MS

Health Communications, Inc.
Deerfield Beach, Florida

Library of Congress Cataloging-in-Publication Data
Middelton-Moz, Jane
  Will to Survive: Affirming the Positive Power of the Human Spirit
  by Jane Middelton-Moz.
    p. cm.
  Includes bibliographical references.
  ISBN 1-55874-231-X
  1. Co-dependency. 2. Resilience (Personality trait) 3. Resilience (Per-
  sonality trait) in children. 4. Self-esteem. I. Title
RC569.5.C63M5 1992   92-13302
155.2'3 — dc20   CIP

1992 Jane Middelton-Moz
ISBN 1-55874-231-X

Publisher: Health Communications, Inc.
          3201 S.W. 15th Street
          Deerfield Beach, Florida 33442-8190

Cover design by Barbara M. Bergman

 # Dedication

To my family who provide the greatest wealth and joy in my life and a loving circle from which to journey from and return to:

Thank you Rudy, Shawn, Jason, Damien, Forrest, Alex, Bette and Melinda for your compassion, humor, honesty, sharing, support and always your love.

# Acknowledgments

This book would not have been possible without the time, energy, clinical gifts, heart gifts and generous support both personally and professionally of a large number of individuals. I appreciate them more than I can possibly acknowledge in a few words. A sincere Thank You goes to . . .

Rudolph I. Moz, my husband, colleague and friend, for his continued support of me personally and professionally and for his help in countless ways during the writing of this book.

My sons Shawn, Jason, Damien and Forrest for their insights, caring, support, humor and objectivity.

My office manager, Diane Laut, who consistently offers me her professional expertise, competence, laughter and personal support. Behind every successful woman is a successful woman and Diane is certainly one.

My editor in Vermont, Ken Carter, who offered not only the most competent professional editorial assistance in the writing of this book, but his continual caring and friendship. And to Mary Carter for her friendship, caring and support in countless ways.

Barbara Nichols, for her expert editorial direction, support and belief in *Will to Survive*.

Marie Stilkind for her final editing, encouragement and support.

Mindi Blaski, Mal Boright, Tara Chotem, Cynthia Churney, Kelly Craig, Gina Delmastro, "G" Johnson, Nancy Mercer, John Setel O'Donnell, Trisha Pearce, Susan Perry, Drorah O'Donnell Setel and Karen Walin whose compassion, sharing, editorial support and insights are evident throughout *Will to Survive.*

Jason Middelton and Cindy Westcott for their creative talents and perspective.

Linda Sanford for her competent work in the area of child abuse and her willingness to write a foreword to this book in the midst of her own hectic work schedule.

Mary Ellen Berry for her compassion, resiliency and willingness to share herself with others.

Deena Hall, Maureen Kennedy, Ed Kleban, Sue Latell, Vernice Wyles-Longhorn, M. Mackay-Brook, Mallery Mackay-Brook, Pat Richards and Jennifer Vasser for their heart gifts and talented creative prose.

Ann Mortifee for her willingness to share her beautiful song, "Born to Win," with my readers.

Bea Shawanda for her friendship, continually effective contributions to the field and for her willingness to share of herself and her stories.

Shawn Middelton and Forrest Middelton for their hours helping me collate the research.

Nancy Wood, J. Ruth Gendler, J. Allen Boone, Mary Fahy, Don Millman and T. Taylor Bruce for their beautiful creative writings.

The numerous authors quoted in *Will to Survive* who have influenced my thoughts. Lorie Dwinell, Frederich Flach, Anthony Storr, Lenore Terr, Alice Miller, Rollo May, Viktor Frankl, Bruno Bettelheim, Nancy McWilliams, George Vaillant and Gail Sheehy, talented clinicians who have continually through their works and teachings, challenged my mind and heart.

Anna Latimer, Elaine Lussier, LuAnn Jarvie, Kit Wilson, Jacquie Hope and Mary Lee Zawadski for their friendship, caring, honesty and humor during times when I thought the book would never be completed.

Peter Vegso, Gary Seidler, Suzanne Smith, Michael Miller, Teri Miller, Milena Ribas and Vicki Pfenniger for their continued warmth, caring and personal and professional support.

The two hundred individuals willing to take the time from their busy schedules to thoughtfully and thoroughly answer the questionnaires and, in some cases, take part in in-depth interviews that served as the foundation for this book.

The staff at Health Communications for providing long hours, talent and creativity in the publishing of this book.

A heartfelt "thank you" to Sal and Evelyn Mineo who continue to give meaning to the words community and neighbor.

Harold and Joy Belmont for their continual spiritual guidance and friendship.

To Roger Straus for his early mentoring and continued friendship.

A very deep and special thanks to my consultees, clients and the participants in my seminars and workshops who continually teach me more about the strength, compassion, and resiliency of the human spirit.

Author's Note

All of the individuals quoted in the in-depth interviews in this book are real individuals. With the exception of Mary (who preferred that her real name be used) all names and names of other family members have been changed and identifying details such as geographical locations and specific occupations have been altered or omitted in order to protect their privacy.

The individuals mentioned in case examples are composites of many adults and children whom I have seen in my 25 years of clinical practice. The experiences of being reared in hurtful and traumatic environments are frequently similar. Any similarity of examples to specific individuals is only a result of these common characteristics.

Special Acknowledgment

To the enormous strength, courage and resiliency of those countless individuals who grew up in traumatic families and environments and continuously exemplify the compassion, creativity and strength of the human spirit and to children everywhere currently surviving painful circumstances.

(A percentage of the author's royalties from this book will be donated to The National Association for Native American Children of Alcoholics (NANACoA) and to Our House, a non-profit organization in central Vermont committed to improving their communities' response to the widespread problem of child sexual abuse.)

Contents

 Foreword

By
Linda T. Sanford
Author of *Strong At The Broken Places, The Silent Children*
and co-author of *Women And Self-Esteem*

It seems nowdays that if you do something twice, you're an addict. If you do something nice for someone, you're co-dependent. And if you don't brutally confront both of these people, you're an enabler.

As I read Jane Middelton-Moz's book, I am reminded of what Albert Camus said: "Life can only be understood backwards but must be lived forwards." Most studies on resiliency are retrospective, relying on adults who today live well, love well, work well, who look back on what made the difference for them. Their lives are understood backwards and every one of us can identify a core of health within ourselves as we look back at our own lives. We can use this insight to help children currently enduring trauma to embrace those spirited and healthy aspects of themselves.

In a well-intentioned effort to both convince everyone of the deleterious effects of childhood trauma and to attempt to manage overwhelming events via the psuedo-science of predicting outcomes, some have erred on the side of "understanding life forwards." They say boy victims of sexual abuse are bound to become sex offenders unless they "break the cycle." Girl victims of sexual abuse are doomed to choose abusive partners and raise a new generation of victims. If you were physically abused as a child, the popular and professional "wisdom" goes, then you will beat your child. If your parent was a substance abuser, then you or a partner will be too. Even if you were the "family hero" and look good on the outside, the pain you may feel on the inside is secondary to the prediction of late onset addiction: *Your* substance abuse probably won't show up until your forties. That is something to look forward to while the first half of your life seems to be going relatively well!

Children are stigmatized first by the trauma at the time and later by stereotypes we have about adult survivors as relentless victims, latent offenders or just plain old miserable people. For a survivor to contend that he or she feels fine or enjoys life is tantamount to heresy.

Just as limiting, some have taken to "living life backwards," often focusing so much on the past that those predictions of doom and gloom come true. Some therapists and survivors believe that if a survivor feels *too* good or lives *too* well, then the parents' abuse must not have been so bad. Misguidedly, the only way to validate the earlier pain is to become a living memorial to it.

So many times, the sex offenders I treat in group therapy have said, "If it weren't for the abuse I went through as a child, I wouldn't be here today." I tell them that there are literally millions of survivors of childhood trauma in this country but only a small minority of them grew up to be sex offenders. There may be many explanations for why they hurt others today but there is no *excuse*. Many insist on holding their parents accountable for hurting them by hurting others and themselves, as if the pain of today somehow proves that pain existed in the past.

Middelton-Moz's focus on creativity, humor and compassion and her belief in resiliency is refreshing in a time when personal fortunes have been made by convincing survivors that any embracing of these qualities is nothing but denial of their trauma, as if both courage and fear, strength and weakness, anger and resolution cannot peacefully co-exist within the same person. It would be wrong to misunderstand a focus on resiliency as implying that trauma builds character or spurs people on to rich and interesting lives. Trauma hurts children. And, as adults, "living well is the best revenge." The two hundred survivors who speak in this book offer us all valuable lessons in living well.

Introduction

When Lorie Dwinell and I began to do workshops for
professionals and later for adults who had been raised
in alcoholic families, our intent was to promote healing by
validating people's early painful experiences without stig-
matizing them in the healing process. At the time, many
professionals were paying little attention to the healthy
adaptation of children from dysfunctional families.

Instead, these adults who entered treatment for depression, relationship difficulties, panic attacks and the
like were given a psychiatric diagnosis. Labels such as
depressive neurosis or anxiety neurosis indicated that
these individuals were not mentally healthy. However, it
was our feeling that rather than having an unhealthy response to a healthy life, the children and adults we were
seeing were suffering the effects of a once healthy adaptive response to an unhealthy life.

In our book together, *After the Tears*, and later in my
book, *Children of Trauma*, the adaptive response of children
from painful environments was presented as healthy.
These children adapted creatively to their situation by
putting their grief on hold. They rarely received validation
or acknowledgment of their painful experiences, nor

support to process their feelings of suffering. Without support and validation, grieving was not possible. Symptoms of delayed grief often appeared in their adult lives, expressed as depression, anxiety, strained relationships and panic attacks.

In treatment it was necessary for the original painful events to be validated so that grief could be worked through. A supportive environment in the form of a safe individual or group was needed to provide them with an "emotional net" that was unavailable in childhood.

In our early work, we talked about 21 characteristics that frequently indicated adults suffering from delayed grief. These included depression, problems forming relationships, lack of spontaneity and panic attacks, to name a few. We suggested that individuals experiencing such difficulties in their current life seek out a safe environment, either with an individual therapist or a healthy support group. The purpose of this environment would be to allow them to move through painful feelings associated with childhood experiences and toward a sense of well-being.

Working through grief opens up a greater range of emotional expression and more choices, a rainbow of colors between black and white. Griefwork is a means to gain freedom from a painful past rather than remaining stuck there.

The starting point for this book is to support validation and release from painful experiences — not to create another disease. The main thrust is to honor survival adaptation, not to view oneself or others with similar life experiences as helpless victims.

My goal is to validate the creativity, compassion and resiliency of the human spirit.

Born To Live

A song by Ann Mortifee/Michel Legrand

We were born to live
Not just survive
Though the road be long
And the river wide

Though the seasons change
And the willows bend
Though some dreams break
Some of us mend.

We were born to give
And born to take
To win and lose
And to celebrate.
We were born to know
And born to muse

1

To unfold our hearts
Take a chance and choose.

We were born to love
Though we feel the thorn
When a ship sets sail
To return no more
Though a door be closed
And we feel the pain
To chance it all
And to love again.

We were born to reach
To seek what's true
To surrender all
To make each day new.

We were born to laugh
And born to cry
To rejoice and grieve
Just to be alive.

We were born to hope
And to know despair
And to stand alone
When there's no one there.

We were born to trust
And to understand
That in every heart
There's an outstretched hand.

We were born to live
To be right and wrong

To be false and true
To be weak and strong.

We were born to live
To break down the wall
And to know that life
Is to taste it all.

Ann Mortifee Management
Box 91679
West Vancouver, B.C.
Canada V7V 3P3
(604) 926-4602

ONE

Thorns Have Roses

Some people are always complaining
that roses have thorns,
I'm forever grateful
that thorns have roses.

Alphonse Karr

When strengths of the human spirit are misdiagnosed as symptoms, it's time to re-evaluate the process of therapy.

With millions of people involved in psychological counseling or groups of some sort, it behooves us — no matter which side of the desk we are on — to raise questions about the efficacy of the treatment we are giving or receiving. Individuals go to groups and to therapists in order to feel better about themselves. If they come away loaded down with new reasons to be embarrassed about their existence, something is going wrong. It is time to question conventional wisdom and to reaffirm our commitment to wellness.

In trying to understand and cope with the complex emotion problems of adults who exhibit dependent or co-dependent behavior, psychologists and the self-help movement have, in recent years, too often emphasized only the defensive symptoms of adults raised in environments of sexual trauma, physical abuse, verbal assaults and belittlement, repetitive lessons of guilt and shame, cultural oppression and dysfunctional alcoholic families.

Viewing oneself or others as defective children, victims, powerless and diseased is not only shaming but is frequently self-perpetuating. Focusing primarily on illness or interpreting life "through a glass darkly" can severely limit an individual's personal development and sense of well-being.

Both in my personal and professional experience, I have observed that creative survival skills can be healthy adaptive responses even in the most dysfunctional families or in the most tragic circumstances. One can point to numerous illustrations — concentration camp stories, for one — where humor, courage or compassion transformed an unbearable situation into a triumph of the human spirit.

Instead of looking through the glass darkly, let's turn on a light. As children, we also learned some important *good* skills. Why have the self-help gurus and others in the psychological or recovery industry selectively forgotten the true compassion children can show toward — for example — their pets or other animals, toward their younger siblings, toward anyone suffering pain? When did a sense of well-being, a deeply felt need to contribute to society, and a sincere caring about one's family become symptoms of a disease? What has happened to the respect for the resiliency, creativity and strength of the human spirit.

Without these characteristics, the human race would not survive. Although early traumatic life experiences may often cloud over these qualities, they can be recalled. They can be remembered. They can be strengthened. They aid in restoring us to self-empowerment.

The Co-dependency Myth

The self-help and recovery movements of the past two decades have helped millions of individuals to validate and alleviate the pain caused in childhood through the thoughtless acts, cruelties or addictions of their parents and society. The original focus of treatment was one of education and validation, not blame. The intent was to promote health and support delayed grief work and healing without diagnosing individuals as "sick."

But too often creative survivors of childhood trauma have been labeled victims rather than survivors. Like butterflies pinned in the midsection, many victims have stayed stuck in their misery, using their past as a defense against their future. The effort to heal families resulted, for many, in more blaming and further polarization between the generations.

The original 21 characteristics of delayed grief grew to an endless list of symptoms of a disease called co-dependency. According to Dr. Stan Katz and Aimee Liu:

> Melody Beattie lists 254 separate characteristics, any one of which could theoretically signal co-dependency. This list, which she warns is 'not all inclusive,' includes such critical indicators as 'wish good things would happen to them,' 'think and talk a lot about other people,' 'get frustrated and angry,' 'get confused,' 'advise,' 'gauge their words carefully to achieve a desired effect.'

Authors Katz and Liu go on to say:

> Leaders of the co-dependence movement have institutionalized this practice by, on the one hand, proclaiming that our entire culture is co-dependent and, on the other, asserting that denial is one of the basic characteristics of co-dependence! In their analysis, healthy people do not exist, and claims of health are further proof of the disease.
>
> The co-dependence gurus, in fact, do not want people to perceive themselves as normal, functioning adults but as defective children. 'It's crucial to experience the powerlessness and unmanageability that results from co-dependence,' writes John Bradshaw. 'Fortunately, millions are identifying themselves as co-dependents.'

Imagine, 254 separate characteristics of co-dependency. With a laundry list this long, the entire planet's population would qualify as co-dependent. It is not surprising then to discover that pride in resiliency is too frequently interpreted as shame or denial in recovery.

Although I don't believe that professionals, authors of co-dependency literature or individuals who view themselves as co-dependents wish to be seen as defective children, I do believe the emerging attention on disease, symptoms and powerlessness is more shaming than healing. I believe people can be reconnected to their own inner power.

A New Focus On An Old Issue

A year ago I was in the midwest speaking about my last book, *Shame and Guilt: Masters of Disguise*. My talk was about the ways in which children are shamed in families and in our culture and how shame is carried into adult life, with adults continuing the process of shaming themselves and others.

A man came up to me after the talk and introduced himself. "Hi, I'm a co-dependent, food addict, workaholic and sex addict and I'd like you to autograph my book."

"Hi," I said, extending my hand. "I'm Jane. Do you have a name or just labels?"

There was an awkward silence. Although I had heard people introduce themselves like this a number of times, I had never confronted such an endless stream of labels. Judging from the look on the man's face, he probably had never experienced a response like mine. A few seconds passed, and then we both laughed.

"My name is Bill," he said, warmly shaking my hand. "I guess I never realized how that list sounds. Do you think I might be violating the law of labels? Maybe I missed one!"

"I'm grateful for your sense of humor," I said. "How does it feel to identify yourself by those labels time and again?"

He looked pained for a moment, then laughed again. "I don't know. I've never paid much attention to my feelings about it. I will, though."

"Good. I'd be happy, by the way, to autograph your book. Is there anything special you'd like me to write?"

"Yeah. How about 'To Bill, a man with a wonderful sense of humor.' "

I signed Bill's book, and he thanked me and shook my hand warmly.

The next day, Bill approached me in the hotel lobby.

"Jane, last night I kept thinking about what you said," he began. "I looked at the inscription in the book and something in me felt really proud. I haven't thought about my sense of humor in years, certainly never thought about it with pride. Yet in thinking about it last night, I realized my sense of humor helped me to survive through a difficult childhood.

"But in my support group, my humor has been viewed as co-dependent behavior. You know, a way I avoided feelings. Now I wonder. Sure, it *is* a defense sometimes, but it is also one of my biggest strengths. Denying it would be like throwing the baby out with the bath water."

"It sounds as if you learned something important about yourself," I said.

"There's more," Bill went on. "Yesterday you asked me what I felt when I introduced myself by those labels. Now I know the answer. It's shame. Like when I was a little boy. I tried so hard to do a really good job and all that was paid attention to were the few things that weren't perfect.

"After we talked last night, I thought, 'Wow, the tradition continues; only now I'm doing it to myself.' I'm continuing the shaming where my parents left off."

Bill's statement was a moment of clarity for me as well. In his support group, his wonderful sense of humor had been judged as a symptom of avoidance rather than a sign of his resiliency. In fact, he had verified the experience of many of us in the counseling profession regarding the current focus in much of the co-dependency literature. Self-administered shame and blame seem to be reaching epidemic proportions.

I was reminded of a statement by Frederic Flach in his book, *Resilience:*

> One of medicine's oldest adages is *noli nocere,* which means, 'In the effort to heal, do not do injury.'

In more than 25 years of clinical practice, I have been impressed with the incredible personal power and resiliency of the majority of my clients. Children, as well as adults, had more often than not shown personal *power,* not powerlessness, in adapting to dysfunctional environments.

I have treated survivors of terrifying physical, sexual and emotional abuse; survivors of concentration camps who witnessed the deaths of their family members; and Native Americans who survived horrifying abuse in residential schools, including having their ankles and wrists broken when they tried to run away.

While these children did not have the power to stop the abuse or neglect, they demonstrated enormous personal power in their survival. Yet they came for therapy feeling powerless, shamed. The process of healing, as I saw it, was to validate the pain of the environments in which they lived, validate their feelings and *reconnect them with their incredibly powerful spirit and pride in their resiliency.* I agree with Flach when he writes,

> The strengths we require to master cycles of disruption and reintegration throughout our lives is resiliency; and it is resilience that is at the heart of what we call mental health.

Again I ask, why has pride in resiliency been lost? What factors thwart the passage from a painful childhood legacy to an adulthood alive with the possibility of free choice?

I am increasingly receiving requests from lawyers asking me to validate their clients' painful childhood backgrounds and diagnosed co-dependencies as an excuse for violent or abusive behavior in their current adult lives. These are instances in which behavior patterns learned in childhood have gone unchecked into adulthood. Now instead of demanding accountability for such criminal behavior, our legal system is frequently seeking to justify and reward it by rationalizing it away.

Here is another example of what has become socially acceptable behavior. A few months ago, Julie, a therapist colleague, told me about a workshop she had recently attended where the speaker arrived more than an hour late. The speaker, Dr. X, did not apologize to the group for making them wait. Rather, Dr. X began her talk as if nothing had happened.

During the workshop Julie expressed her feelings about Dr. X's tardiness. What was Dr. X's response? She said, "I'm in my recovery for co-dependency. I no longer have to be perfect. I would suggest you reexamine *your* need for perfection!"

In recounting the experience to me, Julie said, "Maybe I'm not seeing recovery in the right way, Jane, but I thought health was taking responsibility for your own behavior instead of blaming someone else. Shoot, that's what my folks did and I still do. My folks, God bless them, worked through their own issues of shame and they don't blame others for their behavior. Has co-dependency become an excuse for rude behavior?"

Reclaiming the "inner child" does not mean becoming a child. You don't quit your job when you can't afford to because you didn't get time to play as a child. You don't stand by and watch while others get abused because once upon a time you cared for others to the exclusion of yourself. You don't refuse a chair to a person because your teddy bear is sitting in it.

Certainly the losses of a five-year-old can seem disproportionately painful if they have been unresolved in life and are preventing balanced living. But we cannot be five years old again, acting out the child's responses. However, recovery from painful delayed grief can be systematically worked out when one feels safe enough to experience the inner pain, anger, fear and vulnerability of that child — *and here's the significant part* — as well as the balancing aspects of compassion, strength, capability and creativity gained through survivorship.

In truly effective griefwork, we learn to see ourselves more objectively, no longer judging ourselves by the harsh expectations or standards of the "mean giants" of childhood. We do not give up the skills we used for effective survival, throwing out the baby with the bath water, as Bill said. Instead, we learn to honor our survival skills. In the process, we can learn the freedom of choice.

Healing is acquiring or regaining the power of choice. Healing is having a sense of and the ability to operate from one's personal power rather than being bogged down in helplessness. As Martin Seligman in *Helplessness* wrote, "Learned helplessness produces a cognitive set in which people believe that success and failure are independent of their own actions."

The healing process should add to our survival skills and highlight capabilities in developmental areas. For instance, an individual may be incredibly responsible, care for others, be highly ethical and sensitive to the needs of others. But if in the healing process the individual is judged, "You're too sensitive, a workaholic and you haven't learned good emotional boundaries," the result is not the promotion of growth or modeled health. Instead, the individual's creatively developed strengths have been shamed.

Consider the story of Helen. She was four years old when she was abandoned by her mother, never to see her again. (Later, Helen learned that her mother had died six years after leaving home.) Helen and her two-year-old brother were sent to a foster home and did not see their father until Helen got married years later. The children were shifted from one foster home after another throughout the years, frequently being separated from one another.

Helen sought out therapy when her own daughter turned four years old. Her daughter's age had provoked the old repressed pain. Helen had become depressed and said she felt hopeless for the first time in her life. At times she feared she would die of cancer. She grew distant from her husband and was frequently angry with him, believing he was going to leave her.

While working through her grief in therapy, Helen told me that feelings of responsibility and concern for her brother had kept her going through a lot of difficult times in those early years. While some of the families they lived with were caring, there were others who were abusive. As she grew older and more independent, she would try to spend more time with her brother.

After some time in treatment, Helen began to do volunteer work in a children's home. A short time later this work became a steady part-time job. For a while the job was constantly in her thoughts. She reached out to the children in ways she wished she had been cared for. In effect, she reparented herself in the hours she spent with them. She often commented, "I don't know how to explain it, Jane. There really are no words for what I feel. It's like I'm doing this for me and my folks. I used to be angry at myself, then at my folks. Now I just feel a new freedom more and more. I don't know a name for it. But it sure feels good and I just want to share it."

Helen had progressed from weekly to semi-monthly sessions with me, when one day she entered my office looking sad and ashamed. It was hard for me to believe this was the same energetic woman whom I had seen two weeks before.

She stared at the floor uncomfortably as she spoke. "Jane, maybe I should see you every week again. I don't think I'm as healthy as I thought I was. I think maybe I've been fooling myself all along, and you, too."

"How have you been fooling yourself?"

"I've been in denial," she said, looking at her clenched hands. "I convinced myself and you that I'd really been feeling good. I thought things had been going great at home. Todd and I had been talking more. But I've been so involved in work . . . maybe I'm a workaholic. I've been so concerned about my daughter's school . . . maybe I'm too overprotective. If I'm really honest with myself, I'm probably addicted to work, food and Todd, too. I think I've been denying my co-dependency all along. I must have been using all these outside things to avoid my real feelings."

"What are your real feelings, Helen?"

"I don't know, Jane. I thought I had been happy lately."

I looked at her and smiled. "Helen, is there any chance at all that you really are feeling good? Why are you working so hard to convince yourself otherwise?"

Helen told me what had happened in the past week. She had heard a national presenter speak on the topic of codependency, describing symptom after symptom of the "disease" afflicting individuals, couples and society in general. The speaker admonished the audience for being in serious denial if they had any of the symptoms mentioned and were not receiving treatment for their disease. Helen heard that "denial" could cause lifelong problems and could also create difficulties with her husband and children.

At a break in the meeting, Helen mentioned to the woman sitting next to her that she sometimes overworked and could probably stand to lose a few pounds, but that she felt great and was finishing her therapy.

The woman told Helen that a "naive sense of well-being" was one of the symptoms of the "disease" and that either she was "hiding things from her therapist" or possibly her therapist was an "untreated co-dependent as well."

Helen left the group feeling as ashamed and double-binded as she had as a child. If she validated her own feelings, she was in denial. If she believed she had the disease, she was sick.

Helen's early attention on caring for her younger brother was part of her survival. *It was resiliency, not co-dependency.* Her current attention on children with needs very much like her own early needs showed a growing compassion and empathy for the self she was and for children — not a disease.

"I don't think it's your co-dependency we need to work on next session," I said. At that point, one of Helen's important assets emerged, her sense of humor and ability to laugh at herself.

"Really, Jane? What could my problem be? I know, it could be my inability to validate myself under pressure, or — just maybe — my suggestibility," she said, laughing. "Is there a diagnosis for that or do I have to remain forever without a label?"

The story Helen related has become, sadly, all too familiar to me in the last few years. Lorie Dwinell, an author friend of mine, told me about a recent incident that left her speechless. After she had given a presentation on delayed grief, a man stopped her and said, "That was an excellent talk, but you have no business speaking on these issues."

Lorie was taken aback. "Why not?"

"Because you're fat and that means you're still co-dependent!"

What is at issue here? Perhaps the word "co-dependent" should describe a particular relationship rather than the individuals involved. We may exhibit co-dependent behavior in one area or situation, but healthy creative life skills in many other areas. People are multifaced, not one-dimensional. To view individuals as defective children is simplistic. Even the most miserable life is not all doom and gloom. Every now and then everyone experiences a glimmer of sunshine. It is incumbent on the recovery movement and therapeutic counselors to make more of the bits of sunlight shining through the broken shards. It is absurd to narrow the view of the child as isolated from the whole of society while growing up. People's traumatic interactions with some adults, other children or a painful home life are not the only influences on them while growing up. Other, more healthy models — for example, teachers, parents of friends, extended family members — often appear.

To grow into adults with positive self-esteem, children must have a "triangle of needs" satisfied. According to Harper and Hoopes in their book, *Uncovering Shame*, these needs are intimacy, accountability and dependency. Healthy characteristics such as the following will develop if all three sides of the triangle are provided:

> Control of their lives by making changes when they choose to, to be loving, nurturing adults; to accept mistakes as correctable; to know that they are loved; to depend on their parents to help them change and be accountable to standards and values; to accept that changing behavior and attitudes is possible; to take risks and not be afraid to make a mistake since mistakes are seen as one way of learning; to recognize the world as a place that can be trusted; to rely on other people; to be more forgiving of mistakes in others and more accepting of feelings and attitudes in themselves . . . to accept a full range of emotional experiences as desirable and nonthreatening; to appreciate emotional and rational abilities and seek to integrate the two; to own feelings and accept responsibility for how they are expressed; to develop a sense of ethics and spirituality; to set appropriate boundaries both in terms of order in relationships and in terms of interpersonal relating; to respect implicit rules about the flow of information, people, and things in and out of the family.

Although most of the individuals I have seen in therapy over the years did not have many of these needs met by their families while growing up, they have developed amazing abilities to master many of these areas themselves through their own creative resiliency.

This issue is verified in the work of Linda Sanford. Having worked with sexual abuse survivors for the past

15 years, Sanford points out in her book, *Strong At The Broken Places,*

> Widespread media sensationalism has amplified the professional's sense of gloom and doom, by portraying survivors as uniformly deranged, violent, suicidal, chemically dependent or abusive. Despite popular and professional expectations, these survivors have not inflicted trauma on themselves or others. Their thoughts and feelings about childhood trauma are normal, given the abnormality of their experiences. Their problems are not radically different in scope or intensity from those of many others who were not traumatized as children. They leave therapy having resolved the issues that brought them and continue to live useful and rewarding lives.

Of Thorns and Roses

Last year, I received a letter from a woman named Deena. She began the letter after watching a television show on child abuse and then reading a magazine interview with me on shame and guilt. In the interview I said I had made a decision to intervene whenever I witnessed child abuse. I stressed the importance of personal commitment to a sense of community in which people help one another rather than supporting further isolation in our culture.

Deena said that writing was her therapy. Her letter, entitled "I Am the Child," was her way of "giving a voice" to abused children and to let them know she understood. With her permission, here is Deena's letter:

I am the child who has no particular color. I come in all shades. You can find me in your parish, synagogue or temple. I may be the one sitting next to you. I am the child who has dreams of becoming an astronaut, doctor, famous dancer, comedian, even the first woman president of the United States. I keep these dreams to myself because no one is interested in what I think or say, and I don't want them to laugh at me.

I am the child who sits alone in a run-down apartment, cold and hungry, wondering when my mom will come home. I am the child who lives in a big fancy house, hoping my dad never comes home.

I am the child who lives in the streets and calls an abandoned building or a freeway off-ramp home. As tough as it is to survive in the streets, I can't go back because they either don't want me or I can't put up with the abuse. You will find me in every community no matter what size it may be; so you see, I can call anywhere home.

I am the child who is the perfect student. I get good grades and appear happy most of the time, but that pretty smile you see is usually painted on. I am also the child who looks lost, confused and has a hard time concentrating. My mind is somewhere else as I pick at myself or bite my nails until they bleed.

I am the child who cowers down and throws my hands up to protect my face if someone should show any signs of aggression toward me, even if in jest. As this child I won't cry no matter how hard I'm being hit because I've been told to be tough and take my punishment.

I am the child who carries all the bruises on the inside. I've been told countless times I am no good, ugly and will never amount to anything, and I believe them.

I am the child sitting at the dinner table with my stomach in knots waiting for my drunken father. I hate dinner time. I am the child who lies awake at night scared to death he will come into my room and do things to me that hurt and make me feel icky inside.

I am the child sitting in the courtroom after a lengthy trial hearing the verdict of not guilty for the ones who molested me. I guess they didn't believe the words of a child. Yet in my classroom I hear the words our forefathers wrote, things like we are all created equal and have the right to life, liberty and the pursuit of happiness. I would like to ask these men now, did you mean this stuff to be true for children, too? I have to wonder because too many of us are still being abused. In Sunday School we sing "Jesus loves the little children," but why doesn't he love and protect me?

Like the children before, we walk the same path. Sometimes we try to reach out to find someone who will help but for some it's too late.

I am the child who is an adult now, I have the choice to continue on or to break this legacy. I ask for God's strength to help me work through whatever is needed to become a healthy person inside and out and to love myself. Maybe then I can help pave the way to create a different path for the future child to walk down.

This letter is my start.

Over the years, I have received hundreds of poems, pieces of art, letters and cards from people like Deena. Children and adults who express, in so many ways, their love and anger, joy and sorrow, compassion and pain and always, their hope, healing, inner beauty and resiliency.

Two years ago, I received a letter from an eight-year-old child. Her name is Susie.

Dear Jane,

My mom and dad read your books. I liked the pictures in the last one.

My mom and dad don't fight like they used to. They went to talk to a lady after they read your pink book. They told me they were sorry and they both love me. I love them too. It was draggy when I thought I had to choose and sometimes I thought they were fighting 'cause of me. I tried to show them I loved them both but it was hard when they fought.

Thank you for that pink book and the ones with pictures.

By the way. I can draw pictures if you ever need them.

Love,
Susie XO

P.S. My mom and dad know I wrote this so you can write me too if you want. I think I want to be a writer like you when I grow up.

Studying The Personal Power Of Resiliency: Strength Or Symptoms

What would these children, as adults, regard as the strengths that pulled them through difficult periods of childhood? To whom did they turn in pain? What did they consider their greatest supports? Their worst fears and highest ambitions? What was their saving grace as a child? How did they balance anger and resentment with compassion and openness? Were they, as adults, still using the survival skills developed in childhood?

I developed a questionnaire (see Appendix) in order to pursue my study of resiliency characteristics in children of traumatic backgrounds. Two hundred responses were collected, as well as seven in-depth interviews on the subjective impressions of survival adaptation in children.

The accuracy of the subjective responses was tested by interviewing several brothers and sisters who completed the questionnaires. In all cases, they agreed with each other's impressions of family dynamics and coping mechanisms.

The questionnaires, requiring mostly written responses and some multiple choice answers, were given to individuals attending conferences on children of trauma, shame and guilt throughout the United States, Alaska and two locations in Canada. Fifty percent of the conferences were open to the general public, while the other half were geared to professionals in the fields of counseling, health, law enforcement and education. Particular conferences were selected in which the majority of the participants were first-time attendees.

Respondents included 50 men and 150 women with a wide range of ages and occupations. The majority came from families, school systems or communities that were experienced as shaming, traumatic or abusive. A variety of ethnic, racial and cultural backgrounds were represented. The following information was tabulated:

1. *What traumas did you or your parents experience?* Answers included war, death of parents or siblings at an early age, concentration camp, holocaust, sexual abuse, physical abuse, cultural oppression, poverty, cults, religious fanaticism, alcoholism and the like.

2. *What was your greatest childhood fear?* Being abandoned (40 percent); violence or being killed (22 percent); alone in the dark (10 percent).

3. *To whom did you turn when sad or upset?* Kept to myself (75 percent); a pet (20 percent); parents, grandparents or other family members (only five percent — ten individuals).

4. *Did you have fantasy parents? What were they like?* Ninety-five percent had fantasy parents. Common descriptions were: They cared about me, were kind, warm, easy to talk to, patient . . . showed me that they loved me . . . weren't violent . . . were protective.

5. *How would you describe your parents' relationship?* Relationships between parents, step-parent and parent or parental figures were described as "awful, angry, distant or violent" (92 percent). Two respondents commented, "You shouldn't assume that all children had parents. I've felt shame about that most my life." Those statements were well taken. I should not have made that assumption.

6. *My saving grace in childhood was (blank):* (1) humor, (2) compassion, (3) creativity, (4) tenacity or a desire to survive.

7. *The survival skill that I'm most proud of today is (blank):* The same qualities were given by a majority of respondents,

although the top four were in a slightly different order: (1) compassion, (2) humor, (3) perseverance, (4) creativity. The fifth and sixth survival skills and saving graces were listed as "achievement" and "responsibility and hard work."

8. *What survival skills from childhood are you still using today?* (1) humor, (2) compassion, (3) perseverance, (4) hard work, (5) achievement, (6) creativity.

Throughout the process of talking with respondents, both before and after they completed the questionnaires, conducting the in-depth interviews and during my reading of the answers, I was again struck with the incredible resiliency and power of the human spirit. Viktor Frankl's words came back to me from his book *Man's Search for Meaning:* "This striving to find a meaning in one's life is the primary motivational force in man."

The majority of adults I met personally or through the questionnaire bore out the impressions I have received of my clients over the past 25 years. The children and adults who I have known were not powerless. These individuals have not only survived incredible pain, trauma and shaming in childhood but have become adults who, despite difficulties in current life, are compassionate, creative, capable and resilient.

They show humor and courage. They have a desire to heal the pain of past traumas and move ahead into the future. After griefwork they do not see themselves as recovering, but rather as healthy.

Sadly, four individuals expressed fear of losing their support groups if they didn't continue to focus on their "symptoms of co-dependency" rather than the positive activities in their lives. But the vast majority of individuals, at the end of their grieving process, showed compassion and understanding for their parents. They accepted their parents in a new way, without the wished-for qualities they once bestowed upon them in fantasy.

From many people I have heard, "I will never forgive the abuse, but I no longer hate the abuser. I can let go of the anger I used to protect or defend myself. I feel freedom for the first time. Choice is wonderful. I can accept what is offered in a healthy way, and set limits on what is unacceptable."

Many individuals, like Helen, have found healing in contributing significantly to children from similarly painful backgrounds . . . some as a way of completing the process of caring for the child who once was, and some as a way, as one woman told me, "of being a member of the community of the world."

I Climb This Tree Of Life

by Ed Kleban

I climb this tree of life
branches flowing, ever growing
toward the everlasting light
at an exhilarating height
in the heavens high above.

  Crawling up from limb to limb
  among its branches, taking chances
  finding seeds and fruits of knowledge
  in this arbor's splendid college
  among leaves of living green.

I climb this tree of life
throughout the seasons, seeking reasons
for my mind is always questing
even when my body's resting
in the comfort of a bough.

As I climb, I feel the seasons
spin around me and surround me
with their cloaks of changing spirit
sometimes fearing to endure it
but I must grow, or I will die.

I climb this tree of life
and in the summer never slumber
for I'm filled with zest and zeal
pushing upward feeling real
and more alive with every step.

And the view I see around me
of all the other trees astounds me
as I eat fruit at every turn
and want to cherish all I learn
climbing higher every day.

I climb this tree of life
but in the fall my spirits stall
as the days seem somehow longer
I begin to lose my hunger
for the fruits among the leaves.

In the autumn's cool brown splendor
brisk winds swirl the leaves that twirl
concealing every summer thought
I feel alone and somehow caught
knowing winter soon will come.

I climb this tree of life
in winter's cold I now feel old
fearing ice among the branches
feeling all the wind's cold lances
tearing at my heart and soul.

Then I slow my lifelong climb
simply staring, rarely caring
I am filled with all the sorrows
of a thousand lost tomorrows
frozen solid life and limb.

I climb this tree of life
and want to sing when comes the spring
as the sap and blood starts flowing
once again my thoughts are growing
glancing upward through the buds.

As my spirits rise renewed
thoughts are clearing, eyes now peering
seeing all the fruits of life
becoming ripe I leave my strife
and resume my climb once more.

I climb this tree of life
ever growing, slowly knowing
learning throughout all the seasons
of the meanings and the reasons
for each fruit I pick to eat.

And the higher that I climb
I gain laughter, climbing faster
learning winters need not last
I now seek springs as my repast
embracing summers when they come.

TWO

Survival Methods That Work

Courage is not afraid to weep and she is not afraid to pray, even when she is not sure who she is praying to. When courage walks, it is clear that she has made the journey from loneliness to solitude. The people who told me she is stern were not lying; they just forgot to mention that she is kind.

J. Ruth Gendler,
The Book of Qualities

The Lessons We Can Learn From The Child

When I was ten years old I was already an enthusiastic writer. This is somewhat surprising to me now in that I learned when I was in my late twenties that I was dyslexic. I say only "somewhat surprising" because I have also come to see that as a child I was as an accomplished survivor. At the age of ten, I was writing in a journal that I kept buried in my back yard under a tree. I was eagerly writing something called *Man Against Himself: A Battle He Can't Win.* My writing wasn't particularly good then and my spelling was atrocious but in those pages I was both attempting mastery over a painful family environment and turning a life full of sadness into a life that had meaning.

In those earliest pages, eagerly scrawled by a frightened little girl, I was exploring the pain and dishonesty of spoken communication. At ten, I also believed that the result of human beings turning away from the boundless beauty and energy of nature toward the futility of attempting to find personal happiness, worth and meaning in relationships, material objects and money, was suffering and tragedy. I looked back with envy to a time before man could talk.

If I could have chosen a family and a time in history in which to live, it would have been with cave women and cave men who still communicated nonverbally. That little girl I was saw the ability to use intellect and words and the need to accumulate possessions, rather than working together toward a communal survival, as the ruination of mankind.

By the time I was in tenth grade, I had read almost everything Franz Kafka and Nietzsche had written, which was no small task in the little conservative town in which I was living. My mother tore up my copy of *Catcher In The Rye* I'd brought home from Honors English class and when I was 18 she walked out of *Dr. Zhivago,* the movie, because the love scene was "filthy." Still, as a freshman, I read after everyone was asleep or, rather, passed out. I surprised my English teacher that year with a lengthy paper entitled, "Franz Kafka: Blind Man Or Prophet?" Kafka and Nietzsche were the only people, other than perhaps my brother, who really knew what I had learned back then: relationships are both longed for and painful, and living means suffering.

When I was 20, I found my earlier journals and papers buried in a box. I laughed at the writings of that child and young adolescent and felt contempt and shame for what I considered my earlier "ridiculous complaining attitude." I am now awed by the creative resiliency of the child I was. In the past several years, I have developed tremendous respect for my ability as a child to master and survive an extremely confusing and painful environment while developing hope, compassion and a type of meaning in the suffering.

I now see the child I was from a much different perspective. I was a little girl living in an atmosphere of alcoholism, violence and abuse. Yet, from the time I was three, I sought out the world of nature. I felt the timelessness and power of the ocean and found friendship and strength from the trees. I befriended the seagulls that lived near my house, pretending I was one of them. Later when we lived in cinderblock apartments in a small town, the neighbor's magpie became a fantasy grandfather. For years when I thought of those apartments I focused fondly on my memories of the magpie, rather than the drunken brawls or the night the neighbor shot a rifle in the house, almost killing my brother.

As a child, I heard my parents' wars every night. The focus of the battles was always on the difficulties caused by my brother and me or money stresses. I always intervened in those wars when they got too violent. Rules in our house were never the same two days running. My brother and I never knew what was expected. We were shamed and punished for not knowing. My brother was always the focus of my father's anger and ridicule and I was my mother's target. The wars never stopped and neither did the drinking.

Somehow that little girl figured out that life would be better with no words — there would not be the fear of poverty or lack of status that I didn't understand. I also knew, although I'm not sure how, the loneliness and depression my parents suffered daily. I wished daily for some kind of community or extended family like those of olden times that could offer some support and peace to them. I also somehow knew, long before my mother's suicide, that a lot of her rage was due to her sadness and that she had somehow lost a sense of meaning in her life.

I knew from the time I was young that my mother missed her mother. She put fresh flowers under her picture every week. I didn't realize until I was much older that she felt terribly guilty for her mother's death and had lost her own life's meaning then. As a child, I wrote in my journal, "If only Mommy would go for a walk on the beach or in the woods, she'd feel the protection and love that I do in those special places." From the time I was a little girl, I knew my mother wouldn't take those walks. Instead, I earned money even at age 10 to buy her clothes or stuffed animals that I knew would make her stop being angry and feel happy for a little while. I also knew my father wouldn't take those walks. I used to wish they would walk on the beach or in the woods together. Instead, I'd listen to my dad's war stories over and over again and he'd seem to feel a strange powerfulness and for just a little while I'd be released from an inner torture I didn't understand.

As a child, I didn't feel powerless like a victim although I felt helpless to change my parents' lives. I was frightened and sad and I felt a deep sense of guilt for their unhappiness and, when I was older, for their drinking.

I realize today that I took the things they could offer in the way of care and modeling and built on those some special fantasies, creating the parents I needed to raise me to adulthood. They both were hard workers despite their alcoholism. My mother sewed beautifully and baked and my dad cooked. Those were ways they could show care.

From the time I was a young child, I sought out elsewhere the things I needed that my parents couldn't give: the unconditional love of animals, the power and meaning in life from nature. I built a family in fantasy. I created an extended family from animals and the elements in the world of nature around me. I now know that my early writing gave the little girl I was a sense of power and continuity through the exploration of the world inside her.

When I was nine, I met the first adult who really took an interest in me. He was a Native American elder who sincerely showed me that he valued my compassion, caring and love for nature and animals. He valued my spirit and my spirituality. From age nine, I had a real adoptive grandfather who taught me lessons that I have carried with me throughout my life. He supported my internal belief in myself and showed me in so many ways that even though I was abused, I was not a victim. He taught me two important lessons that supported me during many painful experiences: One, that my body may suffer abuse but only I could hurt my spirit; and two, that real survival meant finding the meaning in my life. My elder did what no one had done for me; he validated the pain I was experiencing and supported and validated the survival adaptation that I had already begun. He was, I know now, a powerful therapist although he had no formal education.

When things got really painful and difficult in my young life, I continued drawing from the energy, power and belief in survival that I got from the world of animals and nature around me and I continued exploring my inner world through endless hours, writing in the journal I kept buried in my back yard. I now understand that the writings of that child were an attempt to master the traumas experienced.

The words of Nietzsche stuck in my mind as an adolescent: "He who has a why to live can bear with any how." I now know that he was a child of abuse. Then I only identified with his validation of the feelings I was experiencing.

What Makes The Difference?

When I was in college studying mental illness, I asked myself the same two questions many times. First, how was it that two individuals from seemingly similar backgrounds, responded so differently to the traumas in their lives? Why did one retreat into the world of hallucinations while the other became the therapist treating the first one's psychosis? How did one somehow find a strength and meaning in life while the other did not? Second, was it fair to use the label "mental illness" for the survival adaptation made by a child from a traumatic background? Wasn't that adaptation really more a sign of mental health?

Over the years I have heard clients and others I met through my writing and speaking ask the same questions, only in a slightly different way, "Am I crazy?" They usually were ashamed of the family histories. They presented that their histories provided evidence of the "craziness" they had always feared was just lying in wait under a surface of pseudo-health. It was as though they couldn't possibly be mentally healthy after such a painful, traumatic history. It was as if they thought they were pretending and soon everyone would know. They discounted their strengths and achievements. I remember a comment made by Joe, a man who had lived through extreme physical and sexual abuse in his family, "I was a straight A student — that's a laugh, boy, I really fooled them. I was also considered quite an artist. I don't know how I pulled it off."

"Pulled what off, Joe?" I asked.

"You know, Jane, fooling them. They really thought I was good, you know, and smart, too."

"Joe, is there something you have forgotten to tell me?" I asked, smiling.

"Like what, Jane?"

"Did you cheat on those tests and papers? Did you copy them from someone else or have another person that looked like you take them?"

He laughed, "Of course not."

"Did someone else paint the pictures or sculpt the clay?"

He continued laughing, "No, I did them."

"Well, Joe, I guess then that you're really smart and creative to boot. Is that hard to hear?"

His seriousness returned. "I guess it is. I guess that kid I was really did it. But how? I really thought all my life that I'm some kind of an imposter. I've always discounted what I really accomplished — I guess because I hid my feelings so much.

"I've always felt like such a fake. But those things really weren't, were they? I've never given myself much credit for what I've done. Maybe it's because I thought all these years I must really be crazy under this facade. I haven't painted for years. I should do it again. I guess I've been afraid to test it. I've just focused on the problems I've had in adulthood, you know, like my depression and workaholism."

"What did your family focus on when you were a child, Joe?"

"Problems, particularly mine. I could do a great job, get straight A's and one A-minus but what was seen was the A-minus. Kind of like what I'm doing to myself now."

What About Resiliency?

By far, the majority of individuals I have met through my work, like Joe, showed impressive survival skills as children. Most, however, showed little pride in their resiliency. For the most part, they were not using in the stressful times of their adulthood those very skills that supported them so well as children. Rather than using the skills they had so creatively constructed in childhood to help them through times of depression, anxiety and loneliness, many had learned to devalue their creativity, compassion, humor and tenacity to focus only on the negative characteristics attributed to them as children or the difficulties in current life. In doing so, they duplicate the shaming messages they received as children and ignore their strengths.

As stated so well by Viktor Frankl in *Man's Search for Meaning*,

> There are some authors who contend that meanings and values are 'nothing but defense mechanisms . . .' But as for myself, I would not be willing to live merely for the sake of my defense mechanisms, nor would I be ready to die merely for the sake of my reaction formations.

The field of psychology, and more currently the field of co-dependency, has in many ways contributed to the shaming cycle. When therapists focus on symptoms and a disease model, symptoms become the central concern of clients. It has been my experience that it is rare that the resilient person behind the "symptoms" becomes the focus of conferences, journal articles, self-help literature or even therapy. Very little time, energy and funds have been spent on exploring resiliency factors in childhood despite the fact that most adult children from painful backgrounds clearly show as many strengths in childhood as they do difficulties.

Manfred Bleuler, a Swiss psychiatrist, focused a large part of his career in the study of schizophrenic individuals and their children. In his observations of the children he did not see the high-risk children that many expected. He compassionately portrays what he saw in these children in the following paragraph where he emphasizes their strengths and incredible resiliency:

> Only a minority of the children of schizophrenics are in any way abnormal or socially incompetent. The majority of them are healthy and socially competent, even though there are reasons to suspect adverse hereditary taints in many of them. Keeping an eye on the favorable development of the majority of these children is just as

important as observing the sick minority. It is surprising
to note that their spirit is not broken, even of the children who have suffered severe adversities for many
years. In studying a number of the family histories, one
is left with the impression that pain and suffering has
a steeling — a hardening — effect on the personalities
of some children, making them capable of mastering
their lives with all its obstacles, in defiance of all their
disadvantages.

Through my own life, my clinical work and my current
study of adult children who grew up in traumatic and
shaming environments, I share Dr. Bleuler's observations.
In exclusively focusing on problem areas, such as difficulties in intimate relationships, periodic depressions, anxiety,
panic attacks, etc., we have missed seeing the beauty of
the trees in the midst of the forest, ignoring the lessons
of the healing process that the resilient child has to teach.
It is important to validate the experiences, the pain and
the sadness in order to aid in the grieving of a painful past
but it is also important to support and validate the continued use of the creative personal power and strengths
that brought the individuals into adulthood.

Nancy, a Native American woman in her early forties,
had been removed from her family at age four and placed
in a Christian residential school. This was a common practice inflicted on Indian people throughout the United
States, Canada and Alaska until the early '70s. Nancy not
only experienced the wrenching loss of family and culture
at an early age but was also physically and sexually abused
repeatedly by the adults in charge of the school. She was,
furthermore, repeatedly shamed for her "Indian ways"
and punished for speaking her language. When she was
seven, she had her wrist broken by a teacher for "stealing
a cookie."

When Nancy graduated from the residential school, she returned to her village but found she had changed so much that, "I no longer fit in. I no longer knew my family or Indian ways. I didn't feel accepted. I felt like a stranger. My dad had died in a logging accident when I was seven. I think he had been drinking. After us kids were taken away, my mother started drinking, too. I didn't feel welcome."

Nancy moved from the rural area of her homeland to an urban area several miles away, although she visited home frequently and tried to "recapture" something she had lost. She worked in many different jobs, continued her education at a local college and later married and began raising a family.

When Nancy's oldest daughter turned four, Nancy felt "as though the bottom had fallen out of my life, I couldn't shake it. I began to feel like I didn't want to live."

Nancy went to a counselor in the college and was told that she was "an Adult Child of alcoholic parents." She said that at first she felt excited. She identified with many of the characteristics of Adult Children that she was taught. "It was like I belonged for the first time. I felt a part of the support group. I even talked a little about the residential school, but not a lot. I guess I still feel a lot of shame about that." She said that she was beginning to feel depressed again and was thinking she wasn't "working the program" as well as she could.

Nancy and I talked about the abuse she had experienced as well as the loss of her family and culture at such a young age. At one point I asked her how she had survived the painful experiences.

"Denial, I guess. I don't know. I numbed out a lot, I guess."

"You are such a compassionate and caring woman with a lot of commitment to your own health as well as the health of your family, Nancy. Was there anyone or anything in your childhood which helped you develop that strength and caring?"

Nancy smiled, was silent for a time, and then replied, "You know, Jane, I haven't thought much about my strength or the positive parts of my caring. My support group members think I'm quite a caretaker. I'm always trying to help my mother."

"Well, Nancy, compassion and caring are wonderful qualities in an individual. I don't think a person can care too much. Maybe you just need to give some of that care to yourself sometimes. It isn't compassion and caring that cause difficulties. It's when you can't control the volume on the caretaking, when it's always turned on high. Or sometimes we begin to feel that our caring is more powerful than it is. When people don't change we feel we haven't cared enough. But to have developed the kind of compassion you feel for others, your family and yourself out of all that pain is an incredible accomplishment."

Nancy began to cry. "It is, isn't it? I have accomplished a lot and I do care for myself or I never would have gone to the counselor in the first place. I heard you say in a talk once, 'I hope we never take the care out of caretaking.' I didn't really feel what you meant until now. It feels good to care."

We sat for a long time in silence until Nancy said, "You know, I've been thinking about your question — you know, how I learned all this. Well, it sounds pretty silly . . ."

"What's silly?"

Nancy looked embarrassed. "I think I learned it from a tree," she said laughing uncomfortably.

"A lot of people have learned a lot from parts of nature. I think that's how I survived."

"Really? Wow! Then it's not stupid."

Nancy told me about a tree outside her window in the residential school. She used to talk to the tree and watch it go through harsh winters and still bloom every spring. She said it was an apple tree and she used to sneak apples from it in the fall. Nancy said it was always there no matter what and it taught her she could survive, too.

I asked Nancy if she spent much time walking in the woods now. She said when she first came to the city, she used to love going to the park. Now she was always too busy with her children, her relationship, work, school, counseling and support group meetings. (She attended three a week.)

I asked Nancy if she would consider attending only two support group meetings and on the third day spend some time in the park. She thought about it and finally asked me if I thought that would mean she wasn't working her program hard enough. I told her I thought that time spent in the park might be a healthy part of a program.

Nancy called me several weeks later. She told me that the idea of going to the park was a good one. She said she felt more energy and also began remembering a lot more about that little girl she was. Then she said, "You know what's the best part, Jane? I thought I had nothing to give my daughter. You know, I didn't have a family during my childhood, really, and there were so many things I never learned. Well, I took my little girl to the park with me and taught her about trees. It was wonderful. There's a lot I've got to offer my daughter and I think I'm beginning to feel both the pain and the strength of that little girl I was."

Seeking Comfort

Nancy's story reminded me of a paragraph from Anthony Storr's book, *Solitude*.

Anthony Grey recalled being shown a painting by a Chinese friend in which a beautiful lotus flower is growing out of mud. The human spirit is not indestructible; but a courageous few discover that, when in hell, they are granted a glimpse of heaven.

One of the items in my questionnaire was, "As a child, when I was sad or upset, I turned to _____". Three-quarters of the 200 respondents said they "kept to themselves" and another 20 percent said they turned to animals. In reply to "Before I was 13, I got the most comfort from involvement with _____", 75 percent of the respondents said either "animals," "nature," or "reading books." Only 36 of the 200 men and women responding to the questionnaire answered, "people, including parents and extended family."

Most of the individuals in the study, like Nancy and me, turned to nature or animals for comfort as children. Somehow in their world there was more consistency, security, unconditional love and comfort found from the world of animals and nature or the stories in books than from the family, community or extended family. Through this interaction with animals, nature and books, children from painful childhoods found a meaning in their lives.

Viktor Frankl saw a similar comfort experienced by prisoners in Auschwitz during World War II.

As the inner life of the prisoner tended to become more intense, he also experienced the beauty of art and nature as never before. Under their influence he sometimes even forgot his own frightful circumstances. If someone had seen the faces on the journey from Auschwitz to a Bavarian camp as we beheld the mountains of Salzburg with their summits glowing in the sunset, through the little barred windows of the prison carriage, he never would have believed that those were the faces of men who had given up all hope of life and liberty . . . after minutes of moving silence, one prisoner said to another, 'How beautiful the world can be!'

Beatrix Potter, like so many children from painful backgrounds, also found solace, comfort and companionship from nature, animals and writing. She spent her young life alone without the companionship of siblings, peers or — most of the time — her parents. Margaret Lane writes:

> She was never sent to school, did not share her parents' life to any great extent and was given no opportunity of mixing with other children, apart from occasional encounters with cousins. Her parents did not entertain guests at home; the atmosphere was stiflingly respectable; and no attempt was made to meet the needs of children.

Like many other children who grew up in homes and communities that didn't meet the needs of developing children, Beatrix Potter was left to creatively meet her own needs. She, like many of the individuals who answered my questionnaire, turned to animals, nature and, internally, to a wealth of creative energy.

Margaret Lane writes:

> Most of Beatrix Potter's hours were spent without human companionship. But she did manage to acquire pets: a rabbit, a couple of mice, some bats and a family of snails. She had made friends with rabbits and hedgehogs, mice and minnows, as a prisoner in solitary confinement will befriend a mouse.

According to Anthony Storr, Beatrix Potter wrote in a journal, using a code that only she could understand. It was not until she was 17 and a favorite teacher's five-year-old son was sick, that *The Adventures of Peter Rabbit* emerged, complete with beautiful illustrations of animals. Because of the marvelous resiliency of this lonely little girl, the animals that kept little Beatrix company through hours of isolation and loneliness were to become companions and friends not only to Beatrix but to children all over the world.

Now this is what we believe.
The Mother of us all is
Earth
The Father is Sun.
The Grandfather is the Creator
Who bathed us with his mind
And gave life to all things.
The Brother is the
beasts and trees.
The Sister is that with wings.
We are the children of
Earth
And do it no harm in any way.
Nor do we offend the Sun
By not greeting it at dawn.
We praise our
Grandfather for his creation.
We share the same

Jane Middelton-Moz

breath together —
The beasts, the trees,
the birds, the man.

— Nancy Wood (Taos Indians)
from *Many Winters*

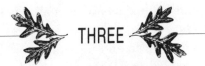

THREE

The Search For Unconditional Love, Courage And Strength

*Those who have the humility
of a child may find again the key to
reverence for, and kinship
with, all life.*

J. Allen Boone,
The Language of Silence

Nature, Animals And Books
As Models In Childhood Survival

Jim grew up on the outskirts of a small developing town in the southwest region of the United States. He was the youngest of five children and the only son. He described his sisters as "spoiled and mean," his mother as "passive and verbally abusive" and his dad as "just plain mean." He said his father was a war survivor who was never "de-warred." Jim said his father grew up in poverty and was considered by the more "uppity" members of the community as "white trash."

"I think my dad had a hard life before the war and the war just topped things off. I think he abused me because I reminded him of himself and he also hated me because I wasn't *macho* enough to suit him. I think he fought all his life against the vulnerability in himself. He hated that quiet side of me. He showered my sisters with lots of attention. I think he may have abused them, you know, sexually. He got them to make fun of me. The oldest, Ann, didn't much. I think Ann wanted to protect me but couldn't stand up to him either. I could see she hated what was going on, though. She died in a car wreck when I was fourteen. I really miss her sometimes.

"Mom was Mexican-American. She got separated from her family early, I don't know how. She never talked about it. Guess it was one of those family secrets. I think she hated herself for being Mexican. I don't know, it's just a feeling I have. She never said much about her culture. I was the darkest of all the kids. Sometimes she tried to shelter me but most of the time she called me names like *stupid, lazy, good-for-nothing* or told me I'd never amount to anything.

"But when we went to town to church — we were Catholic — and I'd feel from the others there that we didn't belong — you know, I'd feel it — she'd be kind and tell me to ignore them. She was always really passive when we'd go to church or to town. Sometimes when Dad would get really mean, she'd tell me to take Matt and get out of there. Matt was my dog. He was only a mutt. I guess I felt a little like a mutt myself back then."

Unconditional Love From A Pet

"Matt was my very best friend. Those were great times. Most days Matt and I would be gone all day. I never felt alone. I had Matt and somehow, being outside in all the beauty of nature, it seemed like we belonged. I felt really special. I felt like the luckiest kid in the world. Matt always showed me so much love and let me know it would be okay.

"We had this special place we went, way up in the mountains. There was this one mountain top where we could see everything for miles around. I felt so connected to something, maybe God. I guess it's no wonder I became a forester and have always had two dogs. I fight for animal rights and environmental rights as if nature and animals were my family. I guess they were. When Matt died, I grieved like some people do for a mother or father. He was everything to me. He taught me so much. I think in some strange way, Matt helped me to love myself."

Jim, like so many individuals I interviewed, suffered enor-
mously as a child. He was abused physically and emotionally
and felt shame in the broader community throughout his
childhood years. Yet the man I met was warm, kind and
showed enormous empathy. He was successful and well-
liked at work, a compassionate father and he worked hard
to make his marriage a good one. His only difficulties
centered around working too much, difficulty following
through on limits, at times, with his children and problems
stating his feelings in his marriage. "I'm still afraid to let
my feelings out sometimes and sometimes I feel 'less than'
others but I'm working really hard on those things with a
counselor and I'm feeling better all the time." According to
the definitions of health formulated by Freud, Adler and
many others — the ability to work, love and have social
interest — Jim was a healthy man.

The Survey

Three-quarters of the individuals in my survey, when
asked who they turned to when they were sad or upset as
a child, said, "I kept it to myself." Twenty percent said they
turned to a family pet. When asked, however, where they
received the most comfort as children, three-quarters of
those responding to the questionnaire answered, "nature,
animals and books." Only 25 individuals out of 200 said
they received comfort from people, be it parents, teachers,
community members or extended family members. Yet I
could only find a handful of articles in the psychological
literature that focused attention on these obviously important factors in the lives of children from painful backgrounds. Rather than focusing attention on supports for
resiliency in children, we have historically focused our efforts and attention primarily on pathology.

Articles by Anne Salomon and Michael Robin speak to the fact that we have ignored the effect pets can have on a child's development, even though animals have always had a place in human life.

Louise Guerney surveyed the coping strategies of 90 latchkey children between the ages of four and twelve and found that interaction with a pet was the second most frequently used strategy. Unfortunately, unsupervised television was number one.

Nature's Message

Although I could find no cross reference between nature and childhood coping, childhood trauma or childhood loss, it was clear that the majority of the individuals in the survey felt that they received the most comfort from the natural environment. Many in their written comments stated that lakes, trees, rivers and oceans gave them modeling, energy, survival skills or a sense of belonging.

Georgia, a very caring woman in her late twenties, told me that her childhood ambition, other than "getting away from home," was to become a veterinarian or a psychologist. "My older brother brought home a psychology book from school when I was in the third grade. I stole it and read it from cover to cover." Georgia did become a child psychologist, well known in her midwestern state for her compassion, creativity and ethics. She was seen by her peers as "a woman who made things happen for children."

Georgia said living in her home was a "nightmare." Her father was alcoholic and her mother was rigidly against alcohol. She said her dad was gone most of the time and her mother always seemed angry. Most of her mother's rage, according to Georgia, had been directed toward her older brother. Georgia said the beatings got so bad once that the neighbors had to call social services and lodge a complaint. "Unfortunately," Georgia said with great sadness, "nothing was ever done."

As a young adult, Georgia realized that her mother's beating of her brother fit a family pattern. She said that her maternal grandfather died when her mother was eight and that her father's mother had died when he was eight. Her mother's brother also died shortly after she turned ten. Georgia said that her father's heavy drinking and her mother's violence toward her brother started when he turned eight, the age that they had experienced such unresolved pain and loss in their own childhoods. Often unresolved grief and loss are re-stimulated in an adult when their own child reaches the age they were when losses and traumas occurred.

Georgia said that her mother was "inappropriately close" to her. "She never allowed me any space or thoughts of my own when I was in her presence. When I had to be with her, it overwhelmed me. Between her smothering of me and the beatings she gave my brother, I ran constantly to the world outside the house. There I found peace, energy, love and the will to live."

Georgia said that she kept her feelings to herself as a child and turned to nature and animals for comfort. "I was building my own fantasy houses in the tops of trees when I was five or six. Even as young as six, I rowed a boat back and forth across a lake near our house for hours on end. My animals gave me unconditional love and I used to think the dew on the grass was medicine sent from God to heal my wounds. It's funny, my family wasn't religious. I never went to Sunday School. But I knew there was a powerful energy in nature that I thought of as the God I had heard adults talk about."

As Georgia talked about the energy, peace and will to live that she had found in nature, I was reminded of a quote from a book I'd recently read by Mary Fahy, *The Tree That Survived The Winter:*

> But mingled with the fear had been that saving, undeniable sense that she had been chosen among the others, had been transplanted with love and conviction to this spot. Often during the cold winter she had questioned the reason, but even while she had trembled with anxiety she had felt an inner voice — a small but steady voice — which remained fluid and alive when everything else had seemed paralyzed . . . she was filled with the realization that her inner life had harmony with the world outside . . . 'I have survived the winter!' she exulted.

Like the tree in Fahy's beautifully written book, Georgia had, in fact, as millions of others like her, "survived the winter." She felt that a lot of her energy and will had been modeled by the natural world around her and her experiences taught her that she was part of that world.

I, like, Georgia and Jim and countless others in my survey, turned to nature as a child. I felt the energy and saw the survival. The ocean gave me a sense of timelessness and a feeling of power that I still can't explain, but I went there as often as I could to recapture that energy and sense of belonging. The trees also gave me that energy as well as providing a sense of survival as I saw them move from winter to spring.

As an older child, my Native American elder directed me to other lessons in nature that I had felt but never had words for. He told me the story of the rock, how it had offered to be the witness to the sadness and grief of mankind. Yet, in that witnessing, the rock remained inde-structible. One day when I was feeling a great deal of pain and sadness from my mother's abuse, my elder showed me the jumping cactus that was in abundance in the desert in summer. He directed me to the very fragile root that trailed along the grass and showed the prickly cactus that shot out at you if you stepped on that root. As young as I was, I realized the similarity between the cactus and my mother's rage and realized that she, too, must have a fra-gile root.

Reading Books, Building A World

Leah, like many others in my survey, did not grow up in an area where she could experience the beautiful world or nature around her. She didn't have a pet as a companion. Her helpmates were books.

Leah was born in Europe after World War II. Her par-ents met in a camp for displaced persons in Germany. Both were Jewish survivors of the horrors of concentra-tion camps. Both had lost family members at the hands of the Nazis. Her father had not only experienced the death of his parents but also of his first wife and daughter.

Her parents moved to France when Leah was a very small child. They were very poor and both parents worked hard to survive, emotionally and physically. Leah re-members her early school experience in France. "I was made fun of because of my clothes and because of my language and I couldn't attend school on the Sabbath. I remember very little of my life in France. I do remember walks with my father, early, before my sisters and broth-ers were born; I was said to be the apple of my father's eye. That all changed when I was five or six and after we moved to Chicago."

Leah remembered very little of the trip to America or going through Ellis Island. She remembered vividly, however, her early days of school in America. "Again, my clothes were funny. Again, I couldn't speak the language correctly. I didn't know who Eisenhower was. I didn't know about Hitler. But I was smart and I survived."

Leah remembered her early years as very painful. Her parents were extremely religious, very strict, yet "nothing was ever really explained. I was in constant confusion about what I was experiencing from others in the world and what I was living at home. There wasn't communication in our family. I couldn't talk to my parents about problems. I was terrified a lot of the time. The non-Jews used to pick on my sisters, my brothers and me. They'd beat up my brothers if I didn't protect them. I was just a kid but I was the oldest. My parents didn't understand and they were working constantly just to survive. I know now that a lot of the coldness, pain and rigidity I experienced in our family was because of the horrifying experiences they had in the holocaust. They never talked about the past. It was like they just were frozen somehow."

Leah also said that she lost the early connection she had with her father. "It happened about the time we came to America. I was then the same age his first daughter had been when she died in the camps, although I didn't even know about her until I was in my late forties. There were so many secrets. I really knew nothing about my parents. I don't know if my dad's emotional distance with me was because he never grieved over the other Leah. I was named after her, you know. Maybe he just had to work too hard to make a life here for us. I think he just couldn't let himself feel again after all the pain and torture he went through. I always felt different and there was no one there."

When Leah was five or six, she found the wonders of reading. "In books, I could get away. I never had any toys but I could read. I could be the characters. I learned survival. By the time I was eleven, I was reading six novels a week. I learned about American women and different ways. I learned about ambitions like going to college. I learned about romance. Books talked to me. I also had a friend who read books like I did. We were inseparable during our teen-age years. We talked about everything, our dreams, loves, normal things."

Although it caused great problems with her family, Leah did reach her dreams. Her parents' religious beliefs did not condone higher education for a woman — she never really understood why. Leah became a psychiatrist, specializing in the problems of women in our culture and the traumatic effects of the holocaust. She gives countless hours as a volunteer recording the stories of survivors and their families in order for their stories not to be lost.

Leah volunteers at her children's school and works hard to be a mother who is present and supportive. "I want them to know I'm there and to understand the values and beliefs that are important to their father and me. I don't want them to feel the confusion, pain and loneliness I felt. I want them to play and enjoy life as children and, when they are young adults, to understand the effects of World War II on our people and why it is so important to work for peace. I guess my saving graces as a child were my curiosity, intelligence, pride, stubbornness and perseverance. I guess in many ways I'm like my dad. He was stubborn, too, and proud. He survived the camps and I survived the effects of that horror on both my parents."

The Lessons Of Children's Stories

Two of the items in my survey were "My favorite childhood story or fairy tale was _____" and "Who or what I most identified with in a childhood story or fairy tale was _____." Many of the participants said they were never read to. Most of these individuals were those who listed nature or pets as their saving grace as children and lived in more rural areas. As might be expected, those who listed reading books as their saving grace had a lot to say about their favorite story or tale. Many of these individuals lived in cities rather than in rural areas. The favorite story chosen seemed to have little to do with whether the individual was male or female. The stories chosen most frequently as favorites were *Cinderella, The Ugly Duckling, Snow White, Robin Hood, Rapunzel, Heidi, The Little Engine That Could, The Emperor's New Clothes* and *Bambi.* The following are statements from participants regarding the lessons they learned in the stories.

— "*Cinderella* was my favorite story. I identified with Cinderella, not because she was rescued by the Prince but because of Cinderella's pain and tenacity. I felt out of place and was made fun of by everybody else in my family. I was tough and stubborn like Cinderella in meeting my secret goals. Later in life, I was a female version of the rescuing Prince."

— "My favorite childhood story was *The Ugly Duckling.* I, of course, identified with the ugly duckling. I felt like I was ugly and awful as a child. I never fit in anywhere, at home or school. The ugly duckling survived to be proud and so did I."

— "My favorite story was *Snow White.* I, too, had a stepmother who hated me. I felt like an outsider. I identified with Snow White and her search. Also, the dwarfs helped me identify my own feelings."

— "My favorite story as a child was *Robin Hood.* I identified with the poor who felt powerless. I wanted to grow up and be like Robin Hood and help others like me, in a way that allowed them their self-respect. I did do that."

— "I loved *Rapunzel.* I felt locked up in a tower like she was. She found a way out and so did I."

— "*Heidi* was my favorite story. I was orphaned as a child. Heidi was independent and found beauty all around her in the mountains. So did I. I learned a lot about survival from that story. I read it again and again. Heidi taught me to run barefoot in the meadows."

— "*The Little Engine That Could.* The train believed in itself against all odds. I learned that, too."

— "My favorite was *The Emperor's New Clothes.* It was like a repeat of my family. It was neat because I learned that things are not always as people say they are. I could believe in my own view. It was a child who finally said the Emperor had no clothes. That gave me courage."

— "The saddest story was also my favorite, *Bambi.* My mother died like Bambi's. I always cried when I read it. It helped me to grieve when no one else would listen to me. I identified, of course, with Bambi. I learned also to live again."

Sometimes the characters in books that children read provide them with hope, give models for courage and survival and help them to feel much less lonely. Stories like *The Emperor's New Clothes* aid children in learning to validate what they see and hear, despite the denial around them. Charles Smith writes,

> Heroes can help children work through their real fears. Their efforts to overcome an obstacle or vanquish a threat provide children with a model for confronting their own apprehensions, both in their imaginations and in reality . . . Successful outcomes in stories are reassuring because they send the message that determination and intelligence can successfully oppose danger.

We've seen Georgia turn to nature, Jim to a pet and Leah to reading to cope with pain in childhood, yet there is little or no focus on these areas in the literature. Many adult survivors are not encouraged in their therapy to continue to seek out those areas in their lives that once sustained them through hard periods. They receive little validation of their creativity in survival.

Over the years, several of my clients have asked to bring a pet to a difficult session, particularly when they have needed special comfort in telling me something of their current or past life that they've been terrified to say out loud.

One woman listed her childhood dog as a sibling on her geneogram and was laughed at by a therapist. "She was the only real comfort I had in my life; yet, I learned in that session to feel ashamed of my attachment."

I encourage many individuals to explore those fairy tales and children's stories that had so much meaning as a way of discovering unexplored parts of themselves. Many write fairy tales about their lives and in doing so they can grieve, talk about shame, see their lives in perspective or recognize unseen strengths for the first time.

It is often reassuring to return to those comforting, safe places at difficult times in adulthood. Whether they are returning there in body or in spirit, recapturing that comfort and safety can sometimes provide the security to work through a painful time as well as to feel again the courageous spirit of the child they once were.

By understanding where adults who experienced painful childhoods once turned for comfort and found their resilient strength, perhaps we can understand the materials needed to construct a bridge to today's children experiencing pain in their lives. We might learn as much about resiliency as we have about pathology.

We find countless cases in psychological literature of individuals who have reacted to their painful childhoods by acting out that pain and anger on themselves or others, including their children. But what about those who search out a different path, a more creative and peaceful resolution. I am reminded of a children's book, *The Secret Of The Peaceful Warrior* by Dan Millman and T. Taylor Bruce. It creatively portrays the story of a boy confronted daily by a neighborhood bully. The boy, Danny, learns from an old man, Socrates, how to follow the lesson of the small tree that learns to bend with the wind rather than resist the wind's power — and break. Danny learns to confront the rage and fear within himself and fight back through peaceful means rather than through violence:

> That night, Danny's dreams took him again into a dark cave. Socrates was nowhere in sight, only the shadow figure, blocking his way out. But this time he knew the secret: He didn't run. He didn't fight. He

faced it squarely, his arms open wide, and walked toward the light at the end of the tunnel. And, as he passed through the dark shape of fear, it became transparent, glittered for a moment, then vanished, because no fear can withstand the courage, and love, of the peaceful warrior.

Little Girl In The Purple Dress

by Vernice Wyles from *Eagle's Nest*

From a distance I saw her sitting alone on the stone bench beside the waterfall in the fragrant green forest.

I watched her from a distance for a while to observe her mood. She wore a purple dress, white lace socks, and black shoes. She seemed totally involved in the moment. A complete spiritual being in love with life. She appeared to be waiting for someone. She looked content being in the waiting mode. A purple aura of confidence surrounded her like the purple dress she wore.

As I approached her she began to smile and hold out her arms to receive a hug. She said with excitement in her whole being, "Don't be afraid. I'll take care of you." I hugged her and cried. It was me who was the adult. Her childlike courage touched me deeply. She was the hero child.

FOUR

The Creative Spirit

. . . They do not run away from non-being, but by encountering the wrestling with it, force it to produce being. They knock on silence for an answering music, they pursue meaninglessness until they can force it to mean.

Rollo May,
The Courage to Create

Moving Ahead In Spite Of The Pain

Sally, a somber little girl of seven, walks down the side-walk, her eyes scanning the ground as she walks. Now she bends over and carefully picks up a dead beetle she has spied lying on the grass next to the sidewalk. She may continue walking or she may stop at a neighbor's along the way to acquire an empty match box. She knows Mr. Sams always has some because he smokes cigars. She may take the cold drink offered or she may just say, "No thank you," and continue on to her destination.

When Sally arrives at the vacant lot at the end of her street, she carefully surveys the line of crosses before her and begins digging a hole just big enough for the match box. Now, she pulls a tissue out of a little purse she carries on her arm, folds it just right and places it in the match box. Then, oh so carefully, she places the dead insect in its lined casket. She solemnly says a prayer for the beetle, buries it and places a toothpick cross on top of the grave as well as some dandelions.

Next we see Sally return to her sidewalk vigil. If we were to stop her and ask about her behavior, she would tell us she's a nun and that she makes sure all the insect souls go to heaven because God will love them all. She is dressed in a white sheet habit and has tied a tooth pick cross around her neck with a bit of string. Sally will tell us, if we continue to listen, that she has written her very own bible. In it, all things go to a beautiful place called heaven when they die. They are given love every day by a huge person who is far more loving than she is.

Sally's parents tell me that they have been worried about this behavior. They ignored it for a long time, thinking it would probably stop, but it hasn't. Now even Mr. Sams has told them of his concerns. When I ask if they have talked to Sally about the behavior that has concerned them, they say they have, a little. They have been afraid to talk to Sally too much because they're afraid that focusing on the behavior might cause more difficulty. Marge and Bob, Sally's parents, have no idea where all this focus on death has come from. "We are not even practicing Christians, let alone Catholic."

I ask Bob and Marge if anything in particular had happened in the family or at school when this behavior began. They can't think of anything.

The intake form that Sally's parents had filled out said they had no other children, yet it also said there had been two pregnancies. When I asked about this, the room filled with tension and Marge and Bob avoiding looking at each other. Then Bob said quietly, "Well, we had a son before Sally was born, but he died of crib death."

"For heaven's sake, that has nothing to do with it. Why do you even bring it up? Are you always going to punish me? Don't you think I've been through enough?" Marge collapsed in tears.

As I suspected, the death of Sally's older brother did have something to do with it but it wasn't what triggered the behavior in Sally. Rather, it prevented the working through of another, more recent, trauma in her life.

After I got to know Sally and she seemed to be somewhat comfortable with me, I asked her if I might be allowed to attend one of her services. She seemed delighted to let me join her. The next afternoon I attended a service for Mr. Bee. As I knelt down next to Sally in her vacant lot cemetery listening to her prayers, I began to understand, not only Sally's recent behavior but the creativity of a little girl trying to process in isolation the recent death of a classmate as well as her parents' unresolved grief for the brother Sally never knew.

"I'm sorry you had to die, Mr. Bee. I know that you will go to heaven and be loved by God. I'm sorry someone didn't love you enough here. Please God, let Mr. Bee into heaven with Michael and Joey. Also, tell Joey I didn't mean not to love him and especially tell Michael that Mommy and Daddy are sorry. I'll love Mommy and Daddy here for you, God, so they don't have to go, but I'll send more little creatures instead who you can take care of so heaven will always be full."

On our way back to the house, I asked Sally about Michael and Joey. The story that Sally seemed relieved to share made sense of her behavior.

Joey was a classmate who had recently been killed in an automobile accident. His parents had also been killed in the crash. The school, which seemed to be enlightened about griefwork, had held its own memorial service for Joey but Sally had not been allowed to attend because her parents thought it best that Sally be shielded from the pain of childhood death.

Sally, who had never attended a church, had the meaning of death explained to her by another seven-year-old classmate. She was told that children die because they are not loved on earth as much as God loves them and they have to die so they can be with God because God gets lonely.

Sally felt terribly guilty because the last time she had seen Joey she had been angry at him for taking her pencil.

To a seven-year-old, that meant she had been the cause of his death. She hadn't loved him.

Sally had gone home to talk to her parents. When she mentioned Joey's death, they had become tense and told her that she needed to "think happier thoughts." Later that night she heard her parents arguing about Michael. She had heard their arguments a time or two before but had never put it together in the same way. She heard them blaming each other for Michael's death. Each thought that if only the other had been there . . .

Sally concluded that Michael must have felt unloved, like Joey, before he had died. Now she felt guilty for Joey, Michael and her parents. Were they loved enough? What if God needed someone else? Sally, like most children her age, felt powerless in the face of death. She also felt tremendous guilt. Her creative solution to the problem put her in charge of those things in her life that she couldn't control nor master through validation and support from her parents.

Frederic Flach speaks to the inherently resilient qualities in an individual who learns to think creatively.

> The creative act does not create something out of nothing. It rearranges, combines, synthesizes already existing facts, ideas and frames of reference . . . The creative act clearly adheres to the law of disruption and reintegration.

Sally, like many adults and children I have met in my work, had the ability to reintegrate disrupting forces in her life and adapt. "In its broadest sense, creativity can be defined as a response to a situation that calls for a novel but adaptive solution, one that serves to accomplish a goal." In Sally's case, the goal was to continue to feel some kind of power in a world where she had come to feel alone and powerless.

It is not surprising that a large number of individuals in my study saw creativity as one of their greatest saving graces in childhood. They felt that they had creatively adapted to very painful childhoods by creating meaning, power, a sense of stability and a feeling of being loved in families and communities where they felt meaningless, powerless, out of control and unloved. As one man stated, "Creativity was my greatest saving grace as a child. I'm not sure now how I did it. I created for myself a meaningful world out of pain and isolation. I created fantasy parents who loved me despite the fact that they were not capable, because of their numbness (they were survivors of Auschwitz), to connect with each other or their children."

A majority of the respondents stated that they created fantasy parents. They bestowed upon the adults responsible for their raising, the characteristics they needed to possess in order to raise children to adulthood. And they, like Sally, took on the required characteristics. One woman said, "It was the saddest day of my life when my mother died. To me, she loved me as I couldn't love myself and protected me from a dangerous world. Now, I know she wasn't there at all except to criticize me and blame me for everything that happened in the family. More than once, my dad abused me sexually when she was in the room. I now know that she was abused as a child, too. I marvel at the creativity of that child I was. I now know I couldn't have survived without those fantasy parents. At least if you believe you're at fault as a child, you have the control. It's amazing. I was really the protector and caregiver all along." Prior to successful griefwork, this woman saw the child as "stupid" and the part of herself that caused the greatest difficulty in her adult life.

Many of us have been taught that creative individuals tend to be unhealthy, perhaps because we have only focused on difficulties with isolation or problems in relationships — circumstances due more to the delayed grief and unresolved traumas in their lives than to their creativity. As Frederic Flach wrote,

> Psychological testing of creative individuals has clearly shown a close connection between creativity and ability to deal with stress . . . Studies have shown that creative people possess a higher than average number of traits commonly associated with ego-strength, such as dominance, responsibility, self-control, tolerance, intellectual efficiency, an openness to feelings and ideas and a wide range of interests.

In her book, *The Untouched Key,* Alice Miller researched the deprived childhoods of several recognized artists including Picasso and Buster Keaton. She explored Picasso's early years in Spain. His mother carefully taught him not to say anything about anything or anyone. His father taught him to paint. "His father's fondest wish was for his son to win the recognition as a painter that he himself, to his sorrow, never had been given. And the son's wish was for his father to love him."

We picture a little boy who was not allowed to communicate verbally but could paint as early as age three. It was at this age that an earthquake hit the city in which his family was living. Miller tells of this little boy being carried through streets strewn with bodies and the wreckage of buildings, a little boy who later, because of small quarters, witnessed the birth of a child.

> The artist is left with his loneliness as the child was with his. Posterity does not concern itself with his trau-

ma but only with his achievement . . . But if we put
everything together — the earthquake and the birth —
the plight of his parents and of the whole city — an
upbringing of seeing but remaining silent — a particular
constellation emerges that was of indelible significance
for this particular individual.

Rollo May, in *The Courage To Create*, feels in Picasso's
works an individual highly sensitive to the changing world
around him. He speaks about Picasso's early work and of
his passionate relationship with human suffering as he
paints peasants and the poor of the first decade of the
century. Then May sees what he calls the "escapism" of
the 1920s in Picasso's portrayal of bathers at the sea.
Finally, comes the progression to the 1940s when his art
is numbered rather than titled.

> As in the novels of Kafka, one gets a stark and grip-
> ping feeling of the individual's loss of humanity. The
> first time I saw this exhibit, I was so overcome with the
> foreboding picture of human beings losing their faces,
> their individuality, their humanity and the predictions
> of the robots to come, that I could look no longer and
> had to hurry out of the room and onto the street.

Whether Picasso was painting the bodies of his early
trauma or the pain and misery of the developing state of
humankind, one thing is clear: he was, through his art,
not only working through his pain, but successfully com-
municating that pain to his viewers. In an interview with
Christian Zervos in 1935, we get a glimpse of the man.
Zervos, concerned about the accuracy of the notes he was
taking in the interview, offered to show them to Picasso.
To Zervos' surprise, Picasso stated that it was not necessary to read or approve the notes. "You need not show
them to me. The essential, in these times of moral misery,

is to create enthusiasm . . . It is enthusiasm of which we have the most need, we and the young." Then, later in the interview Picasso states, "It is not what the artist does that counts, but what he is. Cezanne would never have interested me if he had lived and thought like Jacques-Emile Blanche, even if the apple he painted had been ten times as beautiful. What interests me is the uneasiness of Cezanne, the real teaching of Cezanne, the torments of Van Gogh, that is to say the drama of the man. The rest is false."

Buster Keaton, too, was a creative man with enormous childhood trauma. He was put on a stage at the age of three with his parents. It was found that the more he didn't laugh, despite his funny clothes, the harder the audience would laugh. He was hit repeatedly on stage by his father yet, according to Miller's account, was not allowed to show emotion. This lack of facial emotions became his trademark in the world of comedy.

> In spite of remembering what happened to him, Buster Keaton undoubtedly repressed the trauma of being abused and degraded. That is why he had to repeat the trauma countless times without feeling it, for the early lesson that his feelings were forbidden and were to be ignored, retained its hold on him.

Like those individuals in my survey who created fantasy parents to raise them to adulthood, Buster Keaton saw his parents in a much different light than did Miller. "My parents were my first bit of great luck. I cannot recall one argument they had about money or anything else during the years that I was growing up . . . From the time I was ten both they and other actors on the bill treated me not as a little boy, but as an adult and a full-fledged performer."

Although individuals like little Sally may not be earning wages for their creative resiliency, they are, nonetheless, using their skills to adapt, survive trauma and find a meaning in their life. Consider this poem by eight-year-old Mallery about a time in her life when she felt her parents' sadness and her own power to save them.

Sadness

Sadness falls across the land
like a black sheet.
it destroys the land,
the people die by the hundreds
until the sadness destroys everything
Everything except one girl.
That girl saves her father
and mother.
She saves the land and the people
The people kneel to her
They say she's brave and strong.

Mallery, Age 8

Creativity is a means of mastering trauma, mastering grief, giving a meaning to life, a way of searching for a type of unity and connection. It is a means of expressing feelings that cannot otherwise be expressed and feeling a sense of personal power in a world that otherwise feels powerless.

Thomas Wolfe speaks of the sense of unity and personal power in creativity.

It was a black time in the history of the nation, a
black time in my own life and, I suppose, it is but natural that my own memory of it now should be a pretty
grim and painful one.

Everywhere around me, during those years, I saw
the evidence of our incalculable ruin and suffering . . .

And from it all, there has come in the final deposit, a
burning memory, a certain evidence of the fortitude of
man, his ability to suffer and somehow survive. And it
is for that reason now that I think I shall always remember this black period with a kind of joy that I could
not at the time have believed possible, for it was during
this time that I lived my life through a first completion,
and through the suffering and labor of my own life
came to share those qualities in the lives of people all
around me.

Through my years of clinical practice, I have seen adults
and children readily use their creative skills, whether in
creative problem solving or through such media as writing, painting, drama or sculpture to work through past
traumas or delayed grief.

Josie showed me her trauma through sculpture. I often
keep a piece of clay by each chair in my office. This was
particularly useful to Josie who was a potter and sculptor.
I learned early on that she was well known for a particular
style of lidded boxes. I asked Josie if she could create one
of the boxes with the clay next to her chair. She was
usually quite withdrawn in my office, but at my suggestion, she became quite animated. When I asked her what
she thought her boxes reminded her of, she didn't know.
Then, I suggested that she imagine herself climbing into
the box in order to feel what it was like from inside. She

said, "Sure," but as she continued with the fantasy, she became more and more nervous.

"Don't close the lid, Jane. I mean, I don't have to close the lid, do I? I can't do it. I can't do it."

We continued working with the boxes for a couple of sessions. At the beginning of the second session, Josie told me that she had been having nightmares about being in a box. At the end of the session, Josie remembered her grandfather locking her in trunks as a way of punishing her.

Josie had recreated the scene of her trauma over and over again through her art. The little girl Josie had been, frightened and confined, attempted mastery over and over again. Only in her mastery did she have control of the boxes and the lids.

Joanne, an African-American in her mid-forties, told me that her saving grace in childhood had been her creativity. She grew up in an area where there was still a great deal of prejudice, so much so that as a child, she had to drink from fountains designated for "Colored" people. She said she knew that the other fountains had colder water and one day when she was six, she tried to drink from the "Whites Only" fountain. She said, "The slap I got from Mama wasn't the worst part. It was the terror in her eyes."

She said that during her growing up years, her mother was emotionally sick and her dad an alcoholic. She said her mother was afraid to eat a lot of the time, fearing the food was poisoned and sometimes her dad, otherwise a kind person, would get drunk and shoot up the place. "I think I knew, even then, that things were a lot harder for my folks coming up than for me."

Joanne told me she was fascinated by music and by numbers. She said she taught herself to play every instrument in the school band. She even wrote her own music.

When she wasn't playing or writing music, she was doing mathematical problems. "They kept getting harder and harder and I loved it. I realize now that part of the music was somehow creating my own 'dance.' You know something beautiful that I could create. Nobody could take that beauty away because I made it myself. I also won awards that made my folks proud and less sad. Somehow, their pride in me was also in themselves. Math gave me some control over the universe. Our house was so chaotic. But math, well, that's different. It's right there, so predictable, so orderly. It gave me some power and some meaning. I felt in control of something."

Degas once said, "A painter paints a picture with the same feeling as that with which a criminal commits a crime." Millions are spent on the criminal, the person who either continues to repeat the violence once done to him or acts out on others the rage felt toward an unkind world. Not much energy is spent on understanding the power, sensitivity and resiliency of the child who feels for the powerless or picks up a paintbrush or a pen instead of a weapon. Frederic Flach wrote,

> Being able to think creatively and approach problems in an imaginative way is an inherent part of resilience. Moreover, there is every reason to believe that learning to acquire and practice proven methods of stimulating creativity will substantially enhance our resources to cope with stress.

Years ago, my children, who were all in grade school, used to be invited to birthday parties at a noisy restaurant, one of a chain. These restaurants, I think, were an effort to keep up with what appeared to be a growing need for more and more mechanical stimulation. There were noisy video games and mechanical puppets that sang loud songs.

I figured that either the noise was too much for an adult such as myself or too much for anybody. Anyway, I always waited outside for my children.

On one particular occasion I saw a little boy quietly coloring outside. He was about ten. I sat down next to him and asked what he was drawing and if he was waiting for somebody.

He said it was too noisy inside. He showed me his drawing which was of a boy approximately his age walking in a storm. In the corner was a rainbow and another figure. When I asked about the other figure, he said, "Oh, I don't know if it has a name. It always keeps me company though."

Somewhere in the conversation, he told me that his dad was in the hospital and he didn't think he was going to live. He said his mother had been really upset and he didn't want to upset her more by talking about it. Then, he smiled. "I don't really need to though because I talk to it." He pointed again to the corner of his paper. "I heard this song on the radio and I've thought about it ever since. It says, 'you never walk alone.' I just drew who I think walks with me."

I believe that children and adults in times of stress, grief and trauma, first seek support from others and, if it is not available from them, seek that support from the world outside or inside the self. The greater the pain within, the greater the need to seek support or to create support, harmony and meaning. Says David Aberbach,

> The very process of creation involves searching for things which can (in theory) be found: ideas, inspiration, technique and ultimately the perfection of the whole. Searching is in any case an expression of the normal impulse to explore and create. Bereavement may give a special force and direction to this impulse.

Among artists who have known severe loss, the search for a work or art might be compared with — or, in some cases, even take the place of — the search for the lost person. The attachment to the lost person might thus be displaced onto the work of art.

*It's easier to put
slippers on your feet than to
carpet the world.*

— *Saturday Night Live*
Skit/February 22, 1992

FIVE

The Power Of Humor

*In laughter, we transcend our
predicaments. We are lifted above
our feelings of fear, discouragement
and despair. People who can laugh at
their setbacks no longer feel sorry
for themselves. They feel uplifted,
encouraged and empowered.*

Allen Klein,
The Healing Power of Humor

Seeking Empowerment And Freedom

Many years ago I worked with a young woman who had suffered a great deal of pain as a child and who had been diagnosed as having a psychotic breakdown in late adolescence. She had been in a hospital for several months when she was 17 and had been prescribed heavy doses of medication to alleviate the auditory hallucinations that had plagued her consistently for weeks. During her time in the hospital, she received medication but did not work on the pain and loneliness she had endured in childhood. The hallucinations eventually stopped and she left the hospital.

When I first met Suzanne, she told me that she was suffering from depression but she denied hallucinations. After slowly gaining her trust, I asked her what she had learned during her hospital stay in late adolescence. She looked at me with a tentative smile and said, "Never to talk about my hallucinations." We both laughed. Then she said, more seriously, "Please, Jane, no more medication. The hallucinations come and go and I've become used to them."

Suzanne was very bright and extremely creative. She agreed to talk about her "voices" as they would come back, on and off, during therapy. We slowly began working on the trauma that she had experienced as a child. When the voices came back, she would write at length in her journal about them. We began identifying them one by one as voices, symbolic and real, of particular people in her past. At one point — I can't recall just how it happened — the voices became characters, roles she would act out in my office, some painful but some quite funny. Suzanne had, despite her traumatic past, developed a delightful sense of humor. The voices eventually no longer troubled her and became quite contained in the characters she occasionally acted out.

One day in my office, Suzanne acted out a comedy routine she had written, using her characters and herself. We laughed and laughed during that session. At the end of the session, Suzanne began exploring the possibility of making her writing, which she'd come to love, a career.

"I was always such a shy kid that I wonder if I could actually sell the talent I have. You know, Jane, I don't feel as shy anymore." We agreed to explore the thought more in our next session.

When I left my office after Suzanne's visit, two of my more serious colleagues told me that the laughter in my office was disturbing to them. One remarked, "What do you do in there, laugh therapy?" I was young and thought that I'd done something terribly against the "codes." I thought that perhaps I'd stepped over a line. Maybe Suzanne's laughter was, as they said, resistance but I knew that she'd worked hard on her issues and never lost sight of them. Yet she took care of herself, making sure she never let herself feel so much at any one time that the feelings might overwhelm her.

I later realized that I had learned as much from Suzanne as she did from me — as is often the case when counselors remain open to what the individuals they see can teach them. Suzanne wrote me a letter many years later to let me know that she was very happy and had not experienced depression in years. She said she knew that counselors frequently never get to know, years later, the gifts they had given or how things turned out for those with whom they worked. She referred to those times in my office when she had begun to "make friends" with her voices, to learn about herself and develop confidence in her survival. She told me that she had become a very successful radio personality, was making an income she never would have believed possible, had many friends and was happy in her career and her life.

The lessons? Suzanne learned that she could make friends with her voices, heal a painful past and respect and love the person she had been and was. She could fully use her humor, compassion and creativity. She was no longer the victim of those in her past who had harmed her; she was in charge and had developed a full and productive life. I learned that laughter, as well as tears, has a definite place in the healing process. I had an answer for the serious colleagues who had questioned the laughter in my office: "Yes, I do laugh therapy, as well as exploring the pain, shame, trauma and strengths of our lives. 'In the effort to heal, we must not do further harm.' "

Just What Are You Laughing At?

We receive countless messages as children that are not helpful in coping with the world. Many of the messages we receive refer to a child's developing sense of humor: *Grow up! — Wipe that smile off your face! — What's so funny? — Be serious — Stop acting like a child! — Just what do you think you're laughing at?* Yet, study after study points to humor as one of the most effective coping mechanisms we have. Rod Martin, in *Humor and the Mastery of Living: Using Humor to Cope With the Daily Stresses of Growing Up,* suggests that parents, caretakers, teachers and any adult figures who actively nurture a sense of humor in children may be equipping them with one of the most important coping mechanisms the children could possibly have to get them to and through adulthood.

Freud, in *Wit and Its Relation to the Unconscious*, said,

> No matter how much restriction civilization imposes on the individual, he nevertheless finds some way to circumvent it. Wit is the best safety valve modern man has evolved; the more civilization, the more repression, the more need there is for wit.

In response to "What was your saving grace as a child?" the answer that not only ranked among the top four adaptive styles of coping but also ranked as one of the top four coping mechanisms that survey participants said they were still using effectively today, was "My sense of humor" or "My ability to keep my sense of humor during . . . painful, lonely, traumatic or stressful times."

In Gail Sheehy's research leading to her best-selling book, *Pathfinders*, she noted similar findings. The ability to find humor in stressful situations and times was one of four coping mechanisms used by those individuals who could overcome life's crises in healthy ways. "Humor, like hope, allows one to acknowledge and endure what is otherwise unendurable."

We find more and more books written on the tragic lives of comedians and humorists and how they survived through their humor. Art Buchwald's mother died when he was a very young child. Jackie Gleason's father deserted him. Carol Burnett's parents were alcoholics who fought constantly with each other. Comedian Louie Anderson's father was an alcoholic who shamed him while his mother medicated him with food. In *The Healing Power of Humor* Allen Klein writes,

Charlie Chaplin, too, found solace in humor. Raised
in one of the poorest sections of London, he was five
years old when his father died of alcoholism. After that
his mother went mad. Chaplin used these gloomy memories in his films and turned them into comedic gems.
Who could forget the scene in *Gold Rush*, for example,
where he eats a boiled leather shoe for dinner because
no other food is available?

There is enormous tragedy in the lives of many comedians and others I have met and treated over the years but
through their compassion and humor, their link with others in pain, they have survived.

Many have compassionately given back to their world
as well. As a young adult, Louie Anderson worked with
emotionally disturbed children. Now he says that one of
his greatest pleasures is seeing children and their parents
in his audiences.

When I look out there and see a kid sitting with his
parents, I don't know what more I could ask for. Because when I'm doing my stuff about my mom and
dad, I'm doing stuff about his mom and dad. He can
look at them and say, 'Hey, you're like that.' And they
might be able to say, 'Sometimes I am like that.'

Those I've met who have the ability to laugh during
stressful times and to see their lives in a broader perspective have also been able to cry with compassion when
another is hurt or injured. In the process of their own
therapy, they have learned to cry for their own pain and,
frequently, for the pain of their parents' lives as well.

Steven Sands summarizes well the healthy adaptive
style of individuals who use humor to cope with the frus-
tration and stress of their lives.

We can say that someone with a sense of humor should have that much more leverage in handling complex messages and emotional states. The appearance of humor may signify an increasingly self-observant ego, and the development of new means for transcending emotional dilemmas . . . In providing a moment of self-exultation, humor also offers a brief refreshment to one's self-esteem.

What Is Humor?

Tom greeted me in his usual manner, "Hi, Jane. I hope your mental health is topnotch today because at this moment I need a super-healthy shrink."

"My mental health is fine today. How was your week, Tom?"

"Well, my dog's at the vet, my sister's in the hospital, I just came from the dentist, my shrink is picking this particularly bad month to go on vacation, but, other than that, I'm just dandy."

I had worked with Tom for over a year and he'd always started the session and ended it on a humorous note. Although it might not seem so to some from his entrance, he was also an individual who worked extremely hard in therapy. Approaching painful areas of his life was difficult for him at times and learning to allow his sadness was also hard; he never ran away from the issues that needed confronting for very long.

Sometimes in sessions I would ask him if I needed my sneakers today. It was a metaphor that had been developed for those occasions when Tom used his humor to block, rather than support, the expression of his feelings. When he'd block, I'd confront him. During an early session, he blocked with humor a great deal. Toward the end of the session, he joked, "Sometimes I really run away from my feelings fast, don't I? But, I can be reassured that my shrink can run faster." At that, I replied, "You're right, Tom, I could use some good running sneakers today."

Tom's greeting shows many of the healthy uses of humor. He engaged with me almost immediately. He let me know that he had a bad week and this might be a stressful session. He let me know that he was fearful about my upcoming vacation. He let me know the events in the past week that were troubling him. At the same time, he lowered his stress level by a humorous release. He defused his tension. He gave himself power and freedom; his humor allowed him to view things in a broader perspective, therefore letting him know that he could feel some control in painful situations rather than feeling helpless. Also he was able to release tension and anger through humor. He let me know that our sessions supported him.

In his book, *Adaption to Life*, George Vaillant lists humor as one of four healthy styles of coping, which contribute to the continued development of the individual.

> Humor is one of the truly elegant defenses in the human repertoire. Few would deny that the capacity for humor, like hope, is one of mankind's most potent antidotes for the woes of Pandora's box.

Humor allows balance and can be a regulator for the emotions, letting one get close to difficult feelings while remaining at a safe distance. It also enables an individual to broaden the horizon, to see things from a different perspective. Says George Vaillant:

> Freud's definition of wit — a sudden illumination of truth — is, in fact, true to its etymology (the word is derived from Old English roots for thinking or knowing).

I think of the value of humor in terms of allowing individuals to see themselves from a broader perspective. That "knowing" is a vehicle for releasing tension, stress and discomfort in a safe way and moving from entrapment and powerlessness to power and freedom. An unusual occurrence in my adult life comes to mind.

It happened some years ago during an exceptionally stressful speaking tour. It seemed from the beginning that little had gone right. Planes weren't on time. Hotels didn't have my room reservations. I felt the exhaustion of going from one city to another and the loneliness that often accompanies extended travel away from family, friends and routines.

When I arrived at the third city, I was really tired and just wanted to go to my room. I was actually feeling quite sorry for myself. The check-in line seemed terribly long. I waited 30 minutes before I finally reached the desk and could check in. The bellman was nowhere to be found so I lugged my two heavy suitcases to the elevator, got off at the tenth floor and finally found my room. I was a lock away from sheer pleasure. I opened the door. It was a very pleasant suite. I checked out the bathroom, then the sitting area and finally my bedroom. There, in my bedroom, lying on my bed, was a nude man giving himself sexual pleasure. There were no suitcases in sight and his clothes were nowhere. I took one look at him, said "Damn it" at the top of my voice and slammed the door on my way out.

Once again, I picked up my suitcases — in the state I was in it never occurred to me to leave them in the hall — I went back down in the elevator and again saw the line.

Once again, there were no hotel personnel in sight. Thirty-five minutes later, after standing in line once more, I was face to face with the desk clerk who had previously checked me in. "Excuse me," I said in a voice that I thought was calm, "but there's a nude man in my room, masturbating on the bed. There is no luggage in the room, no clothes, just him."

The woman behind the desk looked at me impatiently and said in a clear voice, "Madam, that's impossible! The room is clear on my computer." Well, that did it. The most rational part of the tirade I unleashed was that I knew a nude man when I saw one. Needless to say, the clerk called security — I'm still not sure if it was to protect herself from me, an obvious lunatic, or to humor me and have security check out my room. The skeptical security guard did, in fact, find the nude gentleman who, as it turned out, was the missing bellman, the one who was not there to carry my luggage.

They cleared out my room and I finally took off my shoes to flop on the newly made bed. News traveled fast throughout the hotel and soon my room was filled with other speakers and the conference manager who hired me. Everyone was upset. My head was pounding with an overwhelming headache, becoming worse by the minute.

The conference manager, whom I liked a great deal, and who had, to that point, remained silent, calmly came over, put her hand on my shoulder, sat next to me on my bed and said in a serious tone of voice, "Jane, I think we may have overlooked the obvious here. Maybe this is what the hotel does instead of putting chocolates on the pillow."

I laughed so hard that I literally cried. This wonderful, caring and humorous woman had done for me what no one yet had done. She at once helped me relieve days of built-up tension, warmly welcomed me in a caring way and allowed me to see the whole situation from a much broader perspective. It was as though I were looking at myself and all that had happened in the past several days illustrated in a *New Yorker* cartoon. My headache went away, I no longer felt irritated and I was able to get a restful night's sleep. I moved from a place of trapped powerlessness to one of freedom.

It is small wonder that in my survey, humor was second only to compassion (altruism) as the preferred saving grace or adaptive style of coping with a painful childhood. Literally thousands of children and Adult Children from traumatic environments have found that the use of humor allowed them a sense of power and freedom in painfully powerless and restrictive environments. Even in horrible circumstances such as captivity in concentration camps and prisoner of war camps, individuals say that maintaining humor aided them to survive.

Victor Frankl, a Jewish survivor of Hitler's Germany as well as a compassionate author and therapist, speaks to the use of survival humor in his groundbreaking work, *Man's Search For Meaning*. He talks of the utter degradation of the prisoners as opposed to the hierarchy in the camps. "The more prominent prisoners, like the Capos, the cooks, the storekeepers and the camp policemen, did not, as a rule, feel degraded at all, as did the majority of prisoners, but on the contrary — promoted! Some even developed miniature delusions of grandeur. The mental reaction of the envious and grumbling majority toward this favored minority found expression in several ways, sometimes in jokes. For instance, I heard one prisoner talk about a Capo, saying, 'Imagine! I knew that man when he was only the president of a large bank. Isn't it fortunate that he has risen so far in the world?' "

Prisoners of war, too, as illustrated by Gail Sheehy, include humor among the top coping mechanisms.

When the 82 surviving crew members of the U.S.S. Pueblo were released in 1967 after 11 months as military hostages in North Korea, evaluations conducted at the U.S. Naval Hospital in San Diego were compared with those of POW's during World War II and the Korean conflict. The survival pattern among the Pueblo men, as noted, paralleled that found in earlier studies of American prisoners of war. Surviving the experience relatively intact depended most heavily upon courage, emotional detachment, eternal hope, the belief in superiority over the enemy, the imagination to have fantasies, the ability to suppress awareness of the ever present fear of death and a sense of humor.

Humor And Physical Health

While doing a search on existing research in the area of humor, I came upon a study suggesting that the use of humor as an adaptive coping mechanism might affect the health of an individual from the first moments of life. Katherine Dillon and Mary Totten conducted a study at Western New England College in Springfield, Massachusetts in 1989 involving the health of breast-feeding mothers and their infants. Their study involved 17 nursing mothers and their babies. Hardiness in infants directly related to the use of humor as a coping mechanism. They found that coping humor in the mothers related to decreased upper respiratory infections in their infants and to Immunoglobulin A levels in the breast milk.

More and more physicians are finding direct correlations between continually high stress levels and the onset of serious illness. Physicians, researchers and writers such as Norman Cousins in *Anatomy of an Illness*, John Diamond in *Your Body Doesn't Lie*, Bernie S. Siegel in *Love, Medicine and Miracles* and Carl Simonton and Stephanie Matthews-Simonton in *Getting Well Again*, not only speak to the correlation between illness, coping styles and emotional outlook, but to the necessity of changing coping styles in order to lower stress levels as a key factor in surviving illnesses such as heart disease, cancer and MS, to name a few.

Norman Cousins perhaps went further than anyone else in actually finding the correlation between laughter, which he referred to as "inner jogging," and the healing process. Cousins suffered from a serious illness of the connective tissue. He realized that there was a relation between serious illness and stress and rightfully concluded that if stress and anxiety could make you sick, then, perhaps, positive emotions could aid in the healing process. He checked out of the hospital where he was and began a regime of vitamin C and laughter. He watched comedy after comedy in bed in the hotel to which he moved. He found that laughter not only caused a decrease in what had come to be constant physical pain but also began to turn the tide in what had been a debilitating illness.

The ability to cry, whether from sadness or laughter, may also, according to recent studies, improve one's health. Mary Peacock, in a 1980 issue of *Ms Magazine*, gives a survey of the then current research on the importance of crying:

> William H. Frey II, a biochemist with the Department of Psychiatry at St. Paul-Ramsey Medical Center in Minnesota, believes that shedding tears rids the body of toxic chemicals produced under emotional stress.
>
> Another indication that crying is a necessary excretory function comes from Dr. Hans Selye, former director of the Institute of Experimental Medicine and Surgery at the University of Montreal, now president of the International Institute of Stress. He said, "We are just beginning to see that many common diseases are largely due to errors in our adaptive response to stress, rather

than by direct damage by germs, poisons or other external agents." Frey goes on to suggest that the social
prohibition against men crying may contribute to their
high incidence of stress-related illness . . . Even the common cold may be related to a failure to cry.

In his later book, *Crying, the Mystery of Tears,* Frey spec-
ulates that tears of laughter, like those of sorrow, may
also rid the body of harmful toxins.

Maintaining Balance In The Healing Process

A number of years ago I was the closing speaker at a
conference on co-dependence. As I stepped up to the po-
dium, I glanced out at the audience and saw 300 sad,
worn, tired faces looking back at me. I thought to myself,
"And these folks are going home?" My closing talk was
supposed to be on shame, which I had doubts about all
along. How can you close a conference on shame? It is not
a particularly uplifting message. So, I did what I usually
do at times like those, I went on instinct. I asked the
audience, "How many of you have gone to every session?"
Three hundred, or nearly that many, tired hands went up.

"Did any of you skip a session, take a walk, go for a
swim, take a tour around town, you know, say, *enough is
enough?*" One hand way in the back went up.

"So, am I correct in assuming," I held the program up,
"that for four days all of you have relived the pain of your
childhoods, heard it, felt, it, slept it, talked it?" Heads
nodded in front of me.

"Then, all I have to say is that what you didn't realize
when you signed up for this conference was that the
conference planners grew up in shaming environments
and, as a result, have little idea of balance in healing. They

think healing can be accomplished in three days of grueling pain." Laughter began to be heard throughout the audience.

"And, maybe more important than shame, you need to work on the suggestible part of your nature that allowed you to be held captive in this painful place for four days." The laughter grew. "If I continue and give a talk on how children are shamed in childhood, we'll definitely need to call a shrink." I changed the course of my talk. We laughed a lot and talked about the need for balance in life. The tension that had been stored up for days was released in laughter that for many turned to tears. Only one woman complained that she had wanted to hear my talk on shame — to her, I gave a free copy of my previously recorded taped book.

I agree heartily with a quote from an interview with Louie Anderson: "I do have one criticism of the recovery movement;" — and I would add, at times, the practice of some psychotherapy — "they take themselves a little too seriously. It is serious and should be taken seriously but there needs to be room for some humor, too."

In *Children of Trauma*, I said that "To stimulate emotions, then block the release of that emotion . . ." produces trauma. To continue to activate the pain of tragically hurtful childhood experience for days on end fits the definition of trauma.

Many of those people who attended the conference had come to a strange environment alone. A large number of individuals went home to little support, particularly no support for delayed grief. Few had "emotional nets." For many participants, the conference could be viewed in much the same way as their childhoods. The focus was the pain of childhood and resulting symptoms carried into adult life. Little attention was paid to validating and making use of the remarkable resiliency traits and safe, comfortable places they had used as children to help them survive, like humor, creativity, music or the world of nature.

Healing from a painful past does not mean reliving it continually. It means reliving the pain with safety and balance while being continually reminded of the creative and beautiful parts of the self that endured and survived.

Mommy, listen —
My dolly's sick.
Yes, I know it's make believe,
But she might die.
I'm afraid she might go away.
Won't you help me worry?
Is it so hard
To make believe you care?

Pat Richards

SIX

Compassion And Altruism

If I can stop one heart from breaking,
I shall not live in vain;
If I can ease one life the aching,
Or cool one pain,
Or help one fainting robin
Unto his nest again
I shall not live in vain.

                              Emily Dickinson

May We Never Take The Care
Out Of Caretaking

A number of years ago, when my four sons were very small, we went to the circus. To them it seemed huge and spectacular. They were young, the oldest only six. To me it seemed a lot smaller and less spectacular than I remembered from 20 years before. They were overwhelmed by all the new colors, smells and pre-show activity. All of them were full of questions about the animals, the shimmering costumes and the clowns.

Holding their cotton candy and popcorn, they sat mesmerized when the grand entrance began. I loved watching the wonder on their little faces as the women and men in dazzling costumes came in riding elephants with their tails entwined. At one point I glanced at my oldest son, Shawn, and I saw sadness in his face. I tried to focus on what he was seeing. It was a clown walking with a scoop behind one of the elephants. He had a bright red costume and bright red smile but he was obviously having great difficulty walking. He was very small, crippled and appeared to be in a lot of pain.

"Mommy," Shawn said sadly, "look at the pain on the face of that little clown. He hurts behind that painted-on smile. Why can't he ride instead of walking? It's not fair."

I felt the tears sting my eyes. I felt not only sadness at the pain he was seeing behind all the magic and colors of the circus life but pride and surprise that he had the sensitivity to see and feel the pain of that little clown. He was only six but had developed compassion, empathy and the ability to really see and feel what many people much older than him sitting under the tent could not. Unfortunately, my answers to his question were not encouraging ones for a six-year-old. Life wasn't always equal nor was it always fair and that was indeed sad.

As we were walking out of the tent, I ran into one of my college professors, a psychologist as well as a priest. He was wearing his clerical clothing and the boys were full of questions. While we were standing talking, the little clown walked by holding the arm of a larger clown. He was still obviously in pain. "Maybe he can get some rest now, Mommy," Shawn said, still saddened by the pain in the man's face. Then he turned to my teacher. "You know that little clown's in a lot of pain. He should have been riding an elephant, not walking all the way around that circle. It's too far. Mommy says life's not always fair."

The next week in class my professor handed me a sheet of paper. He had written a poem for Shawn titled, "The Boy Was A Gentle Man." He told me that he had been struck by such sensitivity from a child and for him it reaffirmed that if children were raised with compassion and empathy, they would develop into compassionate and empathic individuals.

I realized driving home from class that my professor was only telling part of the story. He had hit upon something that I had thought about for many years. It is definitely true that children raised with adults who model compassion and show love and empathy toward them become compassionate human beings. The lessons of compassion and empathy for others are learned in a compassionate environment. A child learns through nurturing, modeling, caring yet firm consequences for negative behavior toward others, praise for empathic behavior, and compassion for self and others.

As stated so well by Isaac Rubin in his book, *Compassion and Self Hate*,

> A child incorporates into his very substance the experience of being cared for and cherished with respect and dignity, and without the stifling and really contemptuous effects of overprotection. If a child is respected and cherished for his own separate identity and individual needs and proclivities, he cannot fail to learn this lesson and to apply it in the service of compassion. The compassionate child has been encouraged to explore and experiment commensurate with his experience and ability, without fear of recriminations for mistakes.

Yet there is clearly another chapter in this story. Throughout my life I had also met countless individuals raised in environments that were painful, abusive and emotionally shaming, yet who consistently showed great compassion and empathy toward others. These individuals, furthermore, were leaders in their communities, working to create a better and more compassionate world for adults and children. In a world that seemed to be moving toward a morality of "everyone for themselves," "the *me* generation" and the accumulation of material objects instead of emotional values, these individuals showed true concern for others without the expectation of material reward or even acknowledgment.

Mary: A Story Of Compassion, Empathy And Altruism

When a little girl or young adolescent woman comes to live at Mary's foster home, she finds a lovingly prepared basket, just for her, filled with soaps, perfume, toothpaste, toothbrush and other personal items. She soon learns that she is given an allowance for clothing and personal needs. Most of the time the foster child is surprised, having lived quite often in other foster residences where she has had to share personal items. Even the toothpaste in some homes was squeezed onto her brush every morning in order not to waste anything. They also find in Mary someone who will listen and validate their pain. Three days a week, Mary drives them to classes or counseling appointments to ensure that they receive the support they need. Mary's husband, Jim, is also supportive of the nurturance needs of each foster child. Mary and Jim meet with other foster parents once a month for mutual support and to discuss needs, successes and problem areas. Mary attends classes two days a week to get her G.E.D.

Mary is 48 and Jim is 50. They have been married for 25 years and have nine children between them. They have also had a total of 32 foster children in their home, primarily girls who have been victims of abuse.

Mary has a great deal of discomfort at times from arthritis and lupus. Yet she says, "God has given me so much. If I were to die today, I'd go willingly. I've had such a full, rewarding and loving life. He gave me wonderful children and grandchildren to cherish, protect and love. I'm a very fortunate woman." This statement of gratitude is unfortunately all too unusual in our world today. It is even more surprising when one considers the painful abuse, neglect and disruption in Mary's early life.

Mary was the fifth of 12 children in a poor family. Although both parents worked, little was given to the children. Mary's father was an abusive alcoholic. He immigrated to the United States when he was young and, according to the history that Mary learned in her adult years, he was also a victim of physical abuse.

Mary's mother was also alcoholic and emotionally abusive. She was raised in an upper middle class environment, although her parents' financial standards suffered greatly during the depression. From things her mother said, Mary suspects that her maternal grandfather was abusive. Her maternal grandparents were very much against the marriage of their daughter to a poor immigrant and disowned her for a long time, early in their marriage. According to Mary, her mother was physically abused by her new husband. She knew little of managing a household with limited finances. Mary felt that her mother's emotional abuse and neglect of her children was a result of her inability to cope and of her anger at having to raise so many children.

Mary's life was disrupted many times before the age of five. When she was only 18 months old, there was a fire in her house and the family was split up. She and another brother were sent to an orphanage. When she was two and a half, she was sent to live with an aunt and uncle who, she said, were her favorite relatives.

She came home briefly at three and a half, but her mother was pregnant with another child, so Mary was sent to another aunt and uncle. This uncle sexually molested Mary. She remembers her uncle telling her to be "a brave soldier" while he was abusing her.

Mary and one of her brothers were sent briefly to a foster home the summer before she entered kindergarten. She remembers sitting on the front steps of the home with her brother while the foster family ate dinner and they went hungry. She said the foster father sexually molested her as well as his own daughters. He was eventually sent to prison, where he died.

To this day, Mary keeps on her bedroom mirror a picture of that little five-year-old that she was. "I love that little girl. I know the abuse wasn't her fault. I just feel a lot of sadness for the pain she experienced." Mary also remembers what she heard over and over again from her older brother who was in the foster care facility: "It will all work out someday. God's spirit runs through us continuously." This brother died when he was 20 in a hit-and-run accident. Mary said she believed he knew he would die young. His death was extremely painful for her but she knew God was still with him.

Mary returned to her parents when she started kindergarten and remained there until she was 14. They were extremely poor, often not eating or eating only popcorn for dinner. Sometimes they would steal food out of the train cars that stopped on the tracks behind her home or from trash cans in the alley. Her father was both emotionally and physically abusive to all the children, although more so to Mary's brothers. He sometimes punished his children by making them kneel on popcorn or by shaving their heads. Her mother sometimes baked but the baked goods were given to her friends at the factory where she worked and not to the children. Her mother told the children that they got the abuse they deserved.

Mary's life at school was no more nurturing than it was at home. The other children teased her constantly, called her names and wouldn't touch her. She even recalls being poked by them with a stick on the way to school. Mary wore boys' clothes — the siblings on both sides of Mary were boys — often didn't have shoes and was made fun of because her sandwich, if she had one, was wrapped in newspaper and the bread she ate often came from a garbage can.

Mary said that she was good in sports and her childhood ambition was to be a Physical Education instructor.
Her most painful school memory was from the fifth grade.
She had won all the athletic competitions that year. She
was going to be given a trophy and was to participate in
the all-school olympics. The trophy was to be presented to
her at a school dance. She felt extremely proud and spent
days preparing for the dance. She took her sister's skirt,
her mother's blue blouse and her brother's socks and made
an outfit.

"I spent hours fixing my hair. I thought I looked great.
When I got to the dance, the kids laughed at me and no
one would dance with me. I was so embarrassed, I ran
home. The next day in school, the P.E. instructor told me
that the faculty had decided that because I couldn't cope
with the children teasing me, they had to take my trophy
back and I couldn't go to the olympics. That devastated
me. It ended my thinking I could achieve something. I
started acting out in anger and with sex. I guess I thought
that was all anyone expected of me. I got pregnant when
I was 14."

Mary was then sent to a youth home for evaluation.
"I'll never forget it. I can picture it exactly in my mind.
After you entered through the front door, there was a
hallway. You turned right or left. The side for delinquent
kids was to the right. That's where I was taken. They
made me strip down in front of other kids and poured
disinfectant on me.

"I was sent to a psychiatrist for an evaluation," Mary
said painfully. "The first question he asked was if the sex
hurt me. Then he asked if I enjoyed it. He wanted to
know if it excited me. He got sexually excited as he asked
me more and more questions. Eventually he wanted me to
fondle him and have oral sex with him. He told me if I

was good to him, he'd make sure I could keep my baby. I later found that he reported that I was sexually promiscuous, should not receive custody of my child and should be put in a reform school and not let out until I was 18. I reported him but no one believed me. They said I just said it because I was in trouble."

Mary was sent to a home for unwed mothers. The father of her child, whom she still loved, visited her every weekend and brought her fruit. "He was the first person to give me girl's underwear and he bought me a beautiful pin that looked like a flower. He wanted the baby and so did I."

But the courts decided otherwise. The baby was taken away. The judge said the child, a little boy, would be far better off with a "good family." Mary said she became enraged at the court hearing and tried to choke the judge. For this action, she was sent to reform school where she stayed until she was 18. She was also forbidden to see the father of her child.

Mary said that although she was still rebellious and had a great deal of rage inside her for the loss of her child, she got back into athletics in the reform school and won many swimming trophies for the school. She also sang in the choir. Mary said, "I love music, especially classical. I could listen to it all day."

While in the school, Mary decided that she wanted to be a nun, although she was discouraged from her goals by the other nuns, who said she was much too rebellious. "I was always having to scrub the chapel floor with a brush because I'd get in trouble for my anger."

Mary said she learned about drugs in the school and also about same sex relationships. "One day I was about to take a shower when I saw two girls fighting in the shower room. I ran to tell Sister Ann, who was my favorite nun. She came back with me, looked in the shower, then walked me back outside. She explained to me that the girls were not fighting, but were, instead, loving each other in a sexual way. Sister Ann explained a lot to me. She took the time to talk with me. She told me that I was extremely creative and could create things with my anger rather than lashing out. Whenever I was angry, I could make something of value. She sent me to sewing classes. Later in my life, I had my own business. I designed clothes for people and customized cars. The lessons I learned from Sister Ann are of great value to this day. I made all of my own children's clothes and decorated my own house. I still sew for my grandchildren."

When Mary left the school, she went back on the street. "I got into drugs and lacked direction. The boy I loved, the father of my child, had married someone else, although we kept in touch. I ended up marrying an abusive alcoholic. After a few years of a very unhappy marriage, I got divorced. The boy I once loved, Jim, had also divorced and we finally got married. He was 26 and I was 23.

"Together we began looking for our first child. We went to the juvenile court worker who told us to stop causing everyone problems. This worker eventually told us that our son had been adopted by a very nice family but had been killed in a car accident at age eight. Jim and I spent years trying to locate his grave. I just wanted to tell him that we didn't give him away."

Over the years, Mary and Jim had many happy times and many struggles. Mary had a cancer at one point; one of their sons had chromosome problems and one of their daughters had a heart attack at age 11.

When Mary was 32, one of her daughters confided that her close friend had been sexually abused. Mary had developed a friendship with a local judge who gave her temporary custody of the young woman. This was the beginning. Mary and Jim have taken over 30 foster children since that time.

When Mary was 45 a judge finally told her that her son was alive, married and had three children. "The judge said we could search for him, with his blessing. I was finally reunited with our first son 30 years to the day after he was taken away. I could finally tell him that we loved him and never wanted to give him away."

In our interview I asked Mary, "What were the things that helped you survive all those early years?" She said hesitantly and modestly, "Somehow my care and compassion for others always gave me a reason to survive. It gave my life meaning. I wanted others not to have to experience what I experienced and I think I learned through caring for others how to care for myself. I wanted to grow up and finally tell my story. It was only a few years ago when I told someone the whole truth.

"The kids in my family also supported each other. My brother was a big support, he constantly reminded me that we would get through it all somehow and that we were not alone. He told me that there was a compassionate God with us always."

Mary said that there were four other people who were kind to her. "Jim, of course, was always supportive. He was also from an abusive home and we understood each other. There was Sister Ann, who taught me so much.

"I also remember another Sister, a teacher in kindergarten. I remember sitting on the windowsill, looking out the window at the other kids playing on the playground. I was crying by myself after being teased. She came up to me, put her hand on my shoulder and said, 'God sent you here, Mary, for a purpose. You are equal to all those other children. You will find out someday that it will all be fine in the end.' I have always remembered that.

"There was also a little boy, Bill, who walked to school with me down that same alley where all the kids teased me and poked me with a stick. He used to defend me. He used to say, 'Stop picking on her. It's not her fault that she's less fortunate and doesn't have what we have. Leave her alone.' I still remember his kindness. I wish I could thank him.

"My love of sports, music and nature also got me through. I loved athletics. I still love music and my house and yard are full of plants of all kinds. My creativity helped me a lot; so did my stubbornness," Mary laughed. "Boy, was I stubborn! I still am. I don't let things get me down. I'm a real fighter.

"You know, I was a good kid, really. All those labels hurt me. I wish they'd stop giving kids labels. I hated the labels. The girls come to me now with labels. Why do they do it? I guess 'cause they get money from the government and without a label, or several labels, they can't get the money."

Altruism

It is easy to understand why Mary cries when she sees children who are hungry, cold, neglected and abused or why she has taken such nurturing care of foster children. She is crying for the child she once was and giving to other children the care and understanding that she so desperately wanted from others in her childhood.

What is not understandable to me is why there are countless studies in psychological literature concerning the children who identify with the aggressors in their lives and who grow up hating and abusing. Yet we find so few studies that focus on children like Mary who identified with the victim and showed compassion instead of hate. Perhaps it's because we need those labels of pathology, as Mary said, to capture funds. Perhaps it's somehow easier to understand the anger a child might have and carry into adulthood and not so easy to understand those who make healthy adaptations from backgrounds of painful abuse. Perhaps children who devote their lives to others don't gain our attention in the same way as the dramatic headline stories of those who injure or kill others.

Nancy McWilliams in her article, "The Psychology of the Altruist," has the same questions:

> It is curious, especially in a discipline devoted to in-depth understanding of human motives, that psycho-analysis has little organized theory about the origins and maintenance of motives to help, heal, save, rescue or better the lot of other people.

Altruism could be defined as unselfish regard for other people, their needs and feelings. One of the earliest writings on altruism as a healthy adaptive defense was by R. Grinker in 1957. He wrote,

> Projection of one's own needs results in altruism. The subject gives to and cares for another and receives gratification by identification with the recipient. However, this is more than a defense . . . it is a learning process, increasing strength and stability in the child's ego. It diminishes the dependence of the child on others and increases his sensitivity, enriches his inner life and facilitates socialization.

Grinker's conclusions agree with my findings as well as the findings of McWilliams, Sheehy and Vaillant. Focusing energy on care and concern for others not only allows children from painful environments to vicariously

give love and nurturing to themselves through giving to
others, defends against abandonment and keeps anger in
check, but also, giving to others strengthens their ego
and positive beliefs about themselves. In giving, the child
also receives.

Caretaking is not only a healthy, adaptive defense but
also a learning process that allows a child to grow into
adulthood with increased positive self-esteem. The child
feels like a good person rather than the bad one portrayed
in their abusive environment. These children, by the standards developed by Freud, Adler and others, meet the
criteria of health. They have the ability to love, to work
and they possess social interest.

Vaillant, Sheehy and McWilliams conducted studies for
different reasons but their results were surprisingly similar. Vaillant wanted to follow through adulthood a population that was considered "healthy" at the time of entrance to college. His subjects were successful college
students. He found that this "healthy" population had con-
siderable problems in coping. He found, however, that the
adaptive styles of a few of his subjects resulted in continued growth and development of the individual. He
found four mature coping mechanisms: altruism, suppres-
sion, anticipation and humor.

> Altruism involves getting pleasure from giving to oth-
> ers what you yourself would like to receive . . . Rarely
> an unalloyed virtue, altruism nevertheless provides a
> protective filter for the most searing emotions. Many
> study members who had defensively denied themselves
> pleasure when young never became completely com-
> fortable with their own passions; but they learned to
> derive pleasure from helping others enjoy the very in-
> stincts that made themselves uneasy.

Sheehy set out to find people she considered "pathfind-ers," those individuals who would stand the best chance of sustaining well-being during crisis periods in life. She wanted to learn more about them and study the qualities and defenses they possessed. Altruism was one of those qualities:

> Altruism is also a familiar quality of a pathfinder, most of whom have a cause or purpose beyond themselves. As a coping device, altruism — being of service to others — not only takes one's mind off the problem but also shores up the ego by making one feel like a good person.

Nancy McWilliams, as stated earlier, began her research because she felt that psychoanalysis had done little to understand those in our culture who had motives to help and heal. She asked everyone she knew for referrals to "do-gooders" they might know or have heard about. They needed to be individuals who repeatedly engaged in help-ing others at a cost to themselves. They also needed to be individuals who were not paid for their altruistic acts and were seen by others as functioning well. She narrowed her study to in-depth interviews of five individuals from a broad range of ages and cultural and ethnic back-grounds. She found individuals like Mary, giving back to needs that they themselves desperately felt as children. She also found a significant loss in the third year of the lives of all the individuals in her study. She discovered that these individuals, like Mary, emulated early models of care such as teachers or baby-sitters. The participants in her study identified early with the victim rather than the aggressor.

> In identification with the victim, a double identifica-tion seems to occur: emphatically with the sufferer, and

wishfully with an idealized nurturer or rescuer who meets the sufferer's needs.

McWilliams found, furthermore, that the only times the individuals in her study experienced problems with depression were when they were somehow prevented from being involved with others in a helpful way.

> All subjects could be appropriately described as compulsive in that they all maintained their self-esteem by doing. In periods in their lives when something prevented them from being involved in humanitarian activities, they reported depression . . . They had the capacity to love, to work (periods of depression or exhaustion were rare and their energies were generally well budgeted) yet it was a particular kind of loving work that sustained them.

Results Of The Questionnaire Concerning Compassion And Altruism

"Compassion for others" was listed most frequently by the participants in my survey as their saving grace in childhood. It was also listed by the majority of participants as the quality they were most proud of in themselves as adults.

Over 60 percent of the 200 survey participants were currently engaged in paid or volunteer jobs directly or indirectly related to their pain in childhood: social workers, psychologists, teachers, counselors for the homeless, sexual abuse counselors, managers of shelters for battered women, police officers specializing in domestic violence, physicians, probation officers, griefwork specialists, diversity trainers, foster care workers, vocational rehabilitation workers, nurses, physical therapists, authors of recovery literature, employment counselors, teachers of English as a second language or teachers specializing in emotionally troubled or handicapped children. There were also interior decorators who made their world more beautiful, even in childhood, as a way of counteracting the chaotic and painful environments in which they were raised.

The responses in another area of the questionnaire showed a further connection between childhood pain and the adult of today. To "If I had time and money, I would contribute to _____," 198 of the 200 individuals responded by saying that they wished to contribute to children and adults currently experiencing the pain they once experienced in childhood years. Individuals who stated that they had been sexually abused wished to contribute to sexual abuse survivors. Those who listed poverty as a trauma experienced in childhood wished to contribute to homeless shelters or directly to families experiencing poverty. Those who experienced marked parental alcoholism wished to contribute to children or adult children of alcoholics. Many stated that they would want to contribute time and finances to working with children to help them learn to like, respect and appreciate themselves. Many participants said that they were already donating time and money to children who had difficulties they themselves had experienced in childhood.

Implications For Healing

If it is indeed true, as my study and the research of others in the field indicate, that identification with the victim, altruism, compassion and taking care of others are not only coping mechanisms that aided children to survive painful environments but also mechanisms that increased self-esteem, then what is currently happening in the co-dependecy and Adult Child movement is indeed a tragedy.

The endless focus on caretaking as pathology shames the most intrinsic part of these individuals. It shames their core self. Coping skills that have been seen by many as the highest level of healthy adaptation are being turned into pathology. That very essence of childhood survival, and indeed perhaps the survival of our communities and world, instead of being viewed with admiration and respect, is shamed. Concern about one's neighbor, the willingness to serve and support fellow human beings is being labeled by many as co-dependent behavior.

I have witnessed the label "co-dependent" applied to individuals like Mary who not only survived extremely painful childhoods but who now continually and compassionately give to others who are suffering the pain they once experienced. This label, if Mary were to own it and believe it, would serve to deny her the well-earned respect that she deserves. Labeling her altruistic behavior as co-dependency would shame her as painfully as she was shamed when her trophy was taken away from her in grade school.

I hope someday to see as much focus in the psychoanalytic, psychological, educational and self-help literature on resiliency characteristics as there is currently on pathology. I hope to see the self-help sections of bookstores lined with books helping individuals to accomplish interdependency rather than endless texts on the symptoms of co-dependency. When there is as much focus in therapy on the healthy skills people have developed for survival as on the "symptoms" they carry from early painful years — only then will true healing take place.

Be Still, Dear One

by M. Mackay-Brook

Be still, dear one,
and listen for
not the words
(for they will surely come)
but the quiet beating of your own heart
not the beating
(for it will surely beat)
but the space between.

Be still, dear one,
and listen for
the love of
your own self
for there you will find
the heart of everyone.

Be still, dear one,
and listen for
the sound of God
for in the stillness
in your heart
she lives.

 SEVEN

Tenacity, Perseverance And The Will To Survive

When the winter is severe
The pine trees in this ancient land
Stay green throughout the year.
Is it because the earth is warm
and friendly?
No, it is because the pine tree has
within itself
A life-restoring power.

Ancient Chinese Proverb

A number of years ago while in Italy I met a man by chance who, I believe, exemplified perseverance, the will to survive and also spirituality in its true sense. It was a summer day and I was walking down a narrow street lined with artists selling their work. I was focused on the beautiful paintings along the street so I saw his works before I saw him. His art had an absolutely unbelievable impact. More than any of the paintings I'd seen that day, his showed multiple levels of meaning. His rivers were alive with intensity, yet serene; his trees full of strength, yet they had a delicate quality that I had rarely seen captured on canvas. The faces he painted were full of emotion yet peaceful, purposeful yet questioning. I was completely absorbed in the stories each painting told.

When I came to the end of the line of paintings, I saw the artist absorbed in a new creation, a series of elaborately dressed dolls in an obviously expensive toy store with a young child dressed in tattered clothing looking at them with huge eyes. The child's face showed desire and awe, yet acceptance.

The artist was sitting with his back to me. He was paraplegic. These extraordinarily beautiful paintings were being created by a brush held in his teeth. When he saw me, or I should say felt me watching him, he carefully laid down his brush and said something in Italian. When I let him know I didn't understand Italian, he spoke to me in perfect English.

"Can I help you? Are you interested in one of the paintings?"

"All of them."

He looked at me questioningly.

"No, no. I don't wish to purchase all of them. I'm just overwhelmed by your superb talent. Every one of your paintings is masterful."

"Are you an artist?"

"Not exactly. I'm a writer and I can't draw more than stick figures."

"Writing is an art. Besides I bet you can. If I can paint" — he tilted his head toward his body — "you can. Somebody probably just told you a long time ago that you couldn't. If you think you can paint, you can. If not, you can't. I learned that early in life. For instance, my body's crippled, but I'm not. What do you write?"

His question led to a lengthy discussion. He introduced himself as Tony. He was Italian but was born in the United States. His injuries resulted from a car accident when he was only five. Both of his parents were killed in the accident. He grew up with relatives who, he said, never really wanted him.

"They felt sorry for me. I think their pity caused me more injury than the car accident. They viewed me as a cripple. I can't tell you how much I hated the way they looked at me. They didn't believe I could do anything but exist in a wheelchair all my life and be fed.

"I spent most of my childhood trying to prove them wrong. In my early twenties I stopped needing to prove anything to people. I guess I didn't need to because I eventually earned respect for myself. My stubbornness saved my spirit. That's what's important. My body is just a suit I wear. It's not me.

"Some people who come by look at me with pity in their eyes. They don't see my art or feel my spirit in each piece. They just see a crippled body. I feel sad for them that they view life in such a narrow way. It will make it difficult for them if they ever lose the use of their body. Some people are so caught up in external appearances that they can't even stand normal aging. They're ashamed to face the world when a wrinkle appears. They run to a surgeon. They are crippled. It's a shame."

Throughout our childhoods we hear adults saying, "Don't be so stubborn. Don't be so willful." Yet tenacity, perseverance, the will to live and stubbornness are exactly what meant survival for many children like Tony raised in shaming and traumatic environments.

Tenacity, stubbornness, perseverance or willfulness were listed in the top four saving graces of questionnaire respondents. All eight individuals with whom I conducted in-depth interviews said that these were among the qualities that got them through hard times. Most of the individuals who completed questionnaires also said they still used that tenacity and willfulness to get them through difficult times today. For many it's what helped them get through their therapy.

Saving Graces

Some of the respondents wrote:

- "My saving grace was my belief that 'I can get through this.' "
- "I was stubborn. I wouldn't succumb to another's opinion of me."

- "I never gave up. I'm a fighter."
- "My ability to fight back was my saving grace; to run in the woods and swim in the ocean, to know there was a meaning in life greater than what was happening in the present."
- "My saving grace was my extreme desire to survive even in horrible situations."
- "An inner courage and belief. I was stubborn about surviving."
- "I never gave up. I just tried harder and harder. I wanted to accomplish something in the world and be the kind of parent my parents couldn't be. I did that, too."
- "My saving grace was my tenacity. I don't know where it came from. I was just always willful, I think, from the moment I was born. I was told I was a mistake all my life. I set out to prove them wrong and I did."

Sheehy also found tenacity and perseverance in those individuals she called pathleaders, those who took an active role not only in surviving and sustaining well-being during painful periods in their lives (pathfinders), but in actually creating changes in their world and aiding others in finding their paths. Some of the individuals she refers to as pathleaders: Mohatma Gandhi, Winston Churchill, Golda Meir, Charles De Gaulle. These people suffered loss after loss in their lives and continued tenaciously toward their goals.

Many of those who have become pathleaders faced a severe test or personal trial during their childhoods. Grappling with it, they resisted accepting an injustice. And in adult life they determined to benefit other people who face similar obstacles. An echo of this form of transcendence is heard in those who overcome life accidents by saying, 'No! I refuse to be defined by my losses,' and who commit themselves to an idea or goal that surmounts their own self-interest.

Sam, an individual who filled out a questionnaire and agreed to an interview, is a leader in his community. He is a teacher who is making a difference with children labeled behavior problems. "One of the things I like about working with these children is that they are as stubborn as I once was and as creative in their survival skills. I have received awards for the programs I have created but it shouldn't be me getting the awards, it should be them. They did it. I hate it when adults think they deserve the credit for what children do."

Sam grew up in a family that was perfectionistic and abusive. He said he could never do anything well enough. When he got a B, it should have been an A. He was punished severely for the slightest infraction. "My dad would hit me and then beat me harder if I cried. He was a war survivor and thought boys shouldn't cry. My mother would make me kneel in a corner with my nose against the wall. She'd set the timer for an hour even when I was three years old. Somehow everything I did was in someway viewed as a reflection on them. If I got a B on a test or made a mistake in a piano recital, it was that I was trying to shame them — and I was punished."

Sam said that something inside him always knew that the problems belonged to his parents and not to him. He said he didn't know how he knew that, he just did. He said his stubbornness got him through.

"I used to pound my fists on the wall in the corner. The timer would be set for another hour but I wouldn't give up. Sometimes I'd be in that damn corner all day. I wouldn't cry no matter how badly I was hit. I knew it would be okay

for me someday — and it is. I vowed that I'd grow up and
raise my own kids to respect and value themselves. I also
wanted to be of value in the lives of children in general. I
think I've done both. Sometimes I'm still stubborn when I
don't need to be, like when I'm in a disagreement with my
wife. We talk it out though and usually laugh. She's stubborn, too. We both work on it. I think it's a small price to
pay for the benefits I've had in my life from my stubbornness. I'm proud of that part of me. It saved my life. Mostly
now I just use my tenacity in good ways."

Sam, like many individuals I have worked with, identified
with that victimized child yet refused to see himself as a
victim. Instead, with compassion, he set out to do a better
job as a parent and also to help other victimized children.

Sam's belief that "things would be okay someday" is
what Viktor Frankl refers to as "tragic optimism."

> I speak of the tragic optimism, that is, an optimism in
> the face of tragedy and in view of the human potential
> which, at its best, always allows for: (1) turning suffer-
> ing into human achievement and accomplishment; (2)
> deriving from guilt the opportunity to change oneself
> for the better; and (3) deriving from life's transitoriness
> an incentive to take responsible action.

The Will To Survive
And Find Meaning In The Survival

Again, there is very little in psychological literature
concerning tenacity, stubbornness and the will to survive.
Tony would probably be labeled obsessive compulsive by
our current day psychiatric pathology model, or a coun-
ter-dependent, controller or workaholic in the co-dependency model. Much of the literature that supports these
qualities as healthy survival and coping mechanisms has

been written by leaders in the psychological fields who also survived the concentration camps in Europe during World War II.

Bettelheim, in his book, *Surviving*, refers to these characteristics as an individual's ability to keep his own face. He quotes a passage from Shakespeare, *Sonnet XCIX*.

> *They are the lords and owners of their faces.*
> *Others but stewards of their excellence.*

Bettelheim applied knowledge gleaned from his extremely painful experience in surviving Hitler's Germany to his later work with children and adolescents who had been labeled emotionally ill. He saw a similarity between the environment of the camps and the environments in which the children he treated grew up. He said that in each case either psychological death or actual death became the adversary. It was an individual's will to survive and the meaning found in that survival that made the difference between life or death.

Bettelheim learned a great deal about perseverance and tenacity in survival by observing his own behavior and that of others in the camps.

> Even the worst mistreatment by the SS failed to extinguish the will to live — that is, as long as one could muster the wish to go on and maintain one's self-respect, then torture could even strengthen one's desire to survive and to remain true to oneself as much as conditions permitted. The actions of the SS tended to make one livid with rage, and this gave one the feeling of being very much alive. It made one all the more determined to go on living, so as to be able someday to defeat the enemy.

This statement by Bettelheim regarding rage being turned into tenacity and the will to survive and "defeat the enemy" reminded me of a poem I recently received, written by a 16-year-old young woman.

> *I was in a family I didn't choose.*
> *Everything I did, I'd lose.*
> *Their hands were hard,*
> *their hearts so cold.*
> *I swore I'd get them when I was old.*
> *So I schemed and planned*
> *and found a way.*
> *That would haunt them*
> *'til their dying days.*
> *I'd work and study*
> *I'd do my best.*
> *I'd put my abilities to the test.*
> *Because the day I'd win the fight*
> *Would be the day my dreams*
> *took flight.*
>
> *Jennifer*

This young woman is an honor student who is also involved in many school and community activities. It is evident in Jennifer's poem, as well as in Bettelheim's statement, that the anger resulting from abusive environments has been turned into productive endeavors and perseverance rather than destructively focused against the self or others.

It's interesting that the repeated themes discussed by Jennifer, Sam and Tony, as well as the statements concerning the survivors of concentration camps, all speak to "winning the fight" and "defeating the enemy," by succeeding, surviving and doing well. They swore to themselves that they would somehow say *yes* to life rather than *no* and would succeed in ways their abusers had failed.

I have seen again and again in clinical practice that it is when this perceived battle is over — when success has been gleaned or prisoners of war have been released — that depression occurs. Unfortunately, many clinicians ignore the original trauma or focus on the reaction formation, depression, tenacity or workaholism as pathology, rather than aiding individuals to work through their very real and justifiable pain and anger while re-enforcing their healthy resiliency.

I have heard goals like the following expressed by many of those I have treated over the years:

- To not be the failure they said I was.
- To succeed in parenting and be a compassionate person.
- To not be like my mother or my father.

Somehow, reaching such goals, fighting for their own integrity and self-worth, proving their abusers wrong and surpassing them, became the very goal that aided them in surviving emotional, sexual or physical abuse. This is how they "won" the battle. Many also identified with the victim and vowed to help others suffering as they had suffered. These goals have frequently provided meaning for their lives. They vowed that they would never allow themselves to believe they were victims but, rather, survivors. Yet there is frequently too little support in the therapy or support group environment for celebrating that survival.

It's amazing how powerful this determination and the meaning attached to it are in relation to survival. We have all known of cases in which those characteristics result in an individual's walking after being told it would never happen or a dying person continuing to live until a particular day, or until the person comes to whom they needed to say goodbye.

An individual's tenacity, perseverance and stubbornness seem to be given birth by the meaning and purpose creatively constructed from painful circumstances. For most, it is a meaning that is filled with compassion and hope for the adults they become as well as for those who represent the child they were. Their anger results in creation rather than destruction. That hope, compassion, purpose and creativity are not only worthy of respect and awe but also of celebration.

Restoring Balance

Sue Latell

Deep inside the Wounded Child,
The Lonely Child, who stands
Arms outstretched — crying
Into the darkness — the emptiness
Is a flicker of hope,
A flame of knowing, of believing
In the power of the Universe —
The Divine Ones — to bring forth healing.

The Winter of her pain tells her
It has been too long,
That she has suffered
Beaten herself in so many ways
That others have witnessed
And waited for her
To find her journey back to the light.

Her hope compels her to place trust
In another to guide her
In facing her grief
And the ugly, angry demons of abuse
That made her believe she was somehow not Holy
No longer a child of God.

She brings her Wounded Child to the other
Through fearful protest
And pleads
To help her align with the beauty
She knows is there.
The beauty she sometimes touches
When she walks in nature
Prays to the Creator
When she watches butterflies,
Listens to the creek
Or witnesses the ocean's waves
Rolling out to eternity.

Over time she learns
Through watching the other
How to be gentle with herself —
Difficult in its novelty
It took a long time to learn.
Slowly she allows the Wounded Child
To believe in the kindness of the other
She breathes in the nurturing
As though reaching an oasis
After too long in the desert.

She remembered that Wounded Child
Always found her strength

In the nurturing of those few
Who seemed to see the light in her
And in the woods and the river
When she spent countless daylight hours
Hunting for crayfish
And knew somehow
That she had come to teach
As she took others to her playhouse classroom
And showed them what she knew.

In relation to the other
She found the safety needed
To receive childhood gifts never received —
To grow beyond what she thought possible.
In giving love to her wounded child,
Her strength was renewed
Encouraged to move on
To live the dream of herself
Fully empowered
The woman she always wanted to be.

She stands proud and confident
Compassionate for herself and others
The wounded child has cried and been heard
As she moves out into her world
She caretakes the memory
Of that wounded child
Whose suffering
Taught her so much about life.

She also envisions
The holy child — the wisdom child
Who is joyous and loving

Who deeply cares
For the suffering of all wounded children.

She gives thanks for those
Who have had the courage and insight
To go before her and clear the way.
She carries forth the gifts
She has earned with dignity and respect —
And makes a silent prayer
To clear a path
For those yet to come.

EIGHT

Celebrating Life, Healing Ourselves And Our World

A tree as great as a man's embrace
  springs from a small shoot;
A terrace nine stories high
  begins with a pile of earth;
A Journey of a thousand miles
  starts under one's feet.

The Tao Te Ching of Lao Tzu

To say that we live in a world in pain and out of balance is indeed an understatement. Some months ago, I was in a major city giving a talk. I watched the local five o'clock news show. The first ten minutes reported stories on murder, rape, sexual and physical child abuse, drug dealing and drive-by shootings. It didn't end there. For another full segment I watched reports of war and unrest in various parts of the world. During the entire news broadcast I did not hear one story of positive community support or interaction. I thought that the stories themselves were painful and appalling. Perhaps because I had just delivered a lecture that morning on childhood trauma, I also focused on another upsetting aspect of the broadcast. It did not air one story of compassion or human sensitivity. I thought of the statement this made about our world — how frightening, particularly for many viewers who are children.

There was no model portrayed of growth, change or hope. I asked myself what a child would do with this constant barrage of negativity, particularly if the child had no supportive adult with whom to watch the show. Stimulating emotions, then blocking the release is a definition of trauma. A few days later, I had my answer.

I was speaking at a conference in another city. I had finished my lecture and was waiting near a television set

in the lobby for a friend. One of the conference participants was sitting in front of the set with her child who
appeared to be five or six. The child was watching TV
while the mother read a book on healing the inner child.
A news program came on similar to the one I'd seen
earlier. The child's eyes were riveted to the set as one
tragedy after another unfolded.

"Mommy, what's a serial killer?" the little girl asked,
gently tugging on her mother's arm, her eyes still fixed on
the screen.

"Be quiet, Holly. Don't you see that mommy's reading?"
The child obediently became quiet. Scenes of war filled
the screen.

"Isn't war scary, Mommy?"

"Holly! What did I tell you?" The mother never looked
up from her reading.

The entire scene was too much for me. I moved to the
chair next to Holly. "Hi, Holly, I'm Jane. Boy, the news can
really be scary sometimes, can't it?"

"Oh, hi, Jane," the mother looked up from her book.
"What luck! I missed you after your presentation. Would
you mind autographing my book?" She reached in the bag
full of books next to the chair.

"I would be happy to autograph your book but first I'd
like to talk to your little girl about the news. Sometimes it
can be quite scary and I wondered what she thought about
it. She seemed to be trying to get your attention and I was
sitting close by, so I thought I might discuss it with her
for a minute."

For several minutes Holly and I discussed what she had
seen and how it made her feel. Then another little girl
and her mother, obviously friends, came to get Holly for
a prearranged swim in the hotel pool.

I told Holly's mother that I could sign her book. She looked at me with apparent shame.

"You know, that's what you were talking about this morning, isn't it? Holly was really frightened and I just kept reading my book. I can't believe it, the book I was reading was on healing my inner child. What about my responsibilities to Holly?"

"Did you feel ignored as a child?"

"Exactly. What a lesson! I've really been focused on myself lately. I'm glad you were here. Thank you, Jane."

The interaction between Holly and her mother is indeed a lesson. The stories portrayed on the news broadcast were terrifyingly real. As stated by Sylvia Hewlett in *When The Bough Breaks:*

> Compared with other wealthy countries, children in the United States are much more likely to die before their first birthday; to live in poverty; to be abandoned by their fathers; to be killed before they reach the age of 25. Nationwide, the incidence of child abuse has quadrupled since 1975.

It is a step in the right direction to begin to verbalize and validate the abuse that is occurring in our world rather than ignoring it. But the sheer portrayal of abuse and violence without models of hope, change, limits or active work toward solutions is also traumatic. It mimics the families in which many of us were raised, where trauma after trauma occurred with no structure in place to neutralize the anxiety or model another way. Unfortunately, too often the places where we go to seek healing are also unwittingly perpetuating the isolation and lack of balance that we once felt in childhood, which were traumatizing, shaming and chaotic.

The self-help and therapeutic movements that began to aid in the process of healing the injuries sustained in shaming, abusive me-centered environments are all too frequently preaching the narcissistic behavior we witnessed growing up. The focus is too often on weaknesses not strengths, problems rather than solutions, self-centeredness rather than interdependency.

Christopher Lasch in his book, *The Culture of Narcissism*, speaks to the issue of perpetuating further isolation:

> The trouble with the consciousness movement is not that it addresses trivial or unreal issues but that it provides self-defeating solutions. Arising out of a pervasive dissatisfaction with the quality of personal relationships, it advises people not to make too large an investment in love and friendship, to avoid excessive dependence on others and to live for the moment — the very conditions that created the crisis of personal relationships in the first place.

A young woman once told me, "First I lost my mother to depression and now I seem to have lost her to the self-help movement. She goes to five meetings and two therapy appointments every week. When she comes home from the meetings, all she wants to talk about is recovery. She and my dad constantly want to read me passages from self-help literature. They told me I was co-dependent with my friends. What happened to just plain living? Why should I be told I'm in denial when my relationships with friends feel good?"

Sometimes I think that the inordinate focus on self that is occurring in our culture may reflect a healthy concern for personal well-being but may also indicate a sense of powerlessness in a world that is perceived as doomed to self-destruct. When all we hear is trauma, again without solutions or healthy models that have made changes in some little corner of the world, it is frightening to focus beyond self. An individual who stops to help a driver in trouble by the road and is killed for his efforts makes front page news for weeks. The thousands of individuals who help others and are rewarded by the gratitude of their fellow human being are never on the front page.

Again, we need balance. It is true that we need to heal ourselves before we can pass that healing along to someone else. But it is also true that we can't responsibly put our commitments, including those to our partners and children, on hold while we heal the child we were. If we do, we will have lost more years and more valuable experiences and memories to the pain of yesterday. Healing is a process. It's a part of life, not life itself.

I once thought of myself as a child deserving of the abuse that was handed down to me. Later, with help and validation from caring and loving people, I saw myself as an abuse survivor. Now, I see myself as a multifaceted human being who has had the experience of having been abused in childhood.

A Compassionate Healing Process

Healing the wounds of a painful childhood involves finding a safe and nurturing environment containing the support for trauma resolution that was not present in childhood. It is not possible to heal the scars of emotional, physical or sexual abuse in isolation. It is also impossible to fully heal in therapeutic environments that deny the realities of child abuse; lack respect for defenses and the process of healing; focus on the beliefs, feelings and realities of the therapist rather than the individual; deny or ignore the strengths and abilities of the individual; or support blaming rather than personal accountability.

Validating Trauma And Its Effect

In order for healing to take place there must be support for an individual to validate the reality and pain of life experiences that were not validated in childhood. Often this involves not only listening and really hearing but also asking questions.

Children were injured not only by the traumas they experienced in childhood but also by the lack of validation in the environment. For instance, the adults who witnessed the shaming of little Mary at the school dance and did nothing became conspirators in the abuse. Furthermore, they completely denied the reality of the abuse by blaming the victim. For decades the realities of sexual, physical and emotional abuse were denied by the therapeutic community. Therapists viewed sexual abuse as a fantasy; physical punishment of a child as part of the growing up process; parental alcoholism as immaterial to a child's development.

I have worked with countless individuals who survived wars, parental suicide, death of a brother or sister in childhood, poverty, fanatically religious homes, physical abuse, placement in foster homes or residential schools, sexual abuse, ethnic or cultural oppression — and who were never asked in past therapy about these experiences, let alone how their lives were affected. One 13-yearl-old girl was referred to a therapist after reporting sexual abuse by her mother and was never asked about the abuse. Besides the individuals who can remember traumatic experiences and are not asked about them, there are countless individuals who, in order to survive, have blocked memory of trauma. Without encouragement, what chance have they of retrieving and putting to rest these crucial memories?

Alice Miller speaks to the lack of support for validation:

> As hard as it is to believe, in the entire world there is
> not one single faculty in which a degree is offered in
> the study of psychic injuries in childhood.

Last year I received a poem from Maureen. She had heard me speak about the effects of childhood trauma and had read my book, *Children of Trauma*. She said she felt validated regarding the traumas she had experienced in her childhood. She gave me permission to print her poem.

They Do Have Names
(a poem for Jane)

I'm not crazy
Know why?
Cause I can tell you the names of what
*   I feel now*
I read it in a book by Jane and she told
*   me too*
She said what I felt was "panic" and
*   lotsa kids feel this*
She said it was cause of my "trauma"
*   when I was small*
So there!
I'm not crazy
Know why?

Cause I don't have to be the way they
*   told me I'd always be*
Alone and stupid
I'm gonna call those things by
*   big names like I seen in that book*
*   and I can prove it to you too.*
You're not crazy either
Know why?
Cause I know you have those funny
*   things in you too*
There's lotsa names and people
*   and books*
If you want we can learn together
Wanna?
Know what?
We're kids of "trauma."
*   Thanks Jane*

Respect For Defenses
Balance In The Healing Process

During the war in Iraq many of my clients reported difficulty sleeping, constant anxiety and depression. For the most part this was a natural reaction. The country was at war and that was traumatic. But the trauma of the war also triggered actual memory and body memory of other traumas experienced throughout life.

For some, however, the reaction was increased by overstimulation. When I asked, "How much are you watching the news?" the answer frequently was that the individual was focusing on the war to the exclusion of all other activities. Some denied themselves sleep, watching the news all night long. In response to my suggestion that it would be showing more compassion for oneself to balance life a bit and limit exposure to a more reasonable number of hours, I would frequently hear the reply, "But Jane, isn't that denial?"

Many therapists, rather than supporting respect for defenses and balance in the healing process, actively assault an individual's mechanisms of protection. These therapies add to the parental statements that we often heard as children, "No pain, no gain."

I once worked with a gentleman who had attended a weekend "Growth Retreat" and was actually reabused in the name of healing. He told the group that he had recently remembered being physically abused throughout his childhood by his father. The group leader chose to help him work through his abuse by having him kneel down in the center of the group while all the men in the group beat him with "anger bats." Needless to say, this was not healing but retraumatization.

Another therapist, in order to "help" her clients experince their "inner child," had them suck baby bottles while they curled up in her lap. Other therapists, without the structure and safety of a gradually formed supportive relationship, take their clients on guided imageries back to their painful childhoods. Some do this with groups of a hundred or more individuals at a time or on national television, without regard for an individual's safety or supportive network. There is little difference between living through a trauma without a supportive, safe environment or *re*living it without one.

Alice Miller refers to such methods of healing as violence.

> The capacities of the human organism to bear pain is, for our own protection, limited. All attempts to overstep this natural threshold by resolving repression in a

violent manner will, as with every other form of violation, have negative and dangerous consequences. The
results of any traumatic experience, such as abuse, can
only be resolved by experiencing, articulation and judging every facet of the original experience within a process of careful therapeutic disclosure. In recent decades,
there have been a number of dangerous attempts to
resolve the consequences of childhood traumas by violent means . . . They have, in many cases, resulted in
even greater flight from the truth by way of new forms
of defense such as addiction and other forms of denial,
for example through political or religious ideologies.

All too frequently in childhood an individual's boundaries, feelings and defenses were not respected but violat-
ed. Many grew up in an atmosphere that denied them the
most basic rights of safety and support. Children were
raised without respect for and patience with the developmental process. They were asked to hurry up, grow up,
or complete tasks they weren't capable of accomplishing.
A therapy process will injure rather than heal if it mimics
intrusive violation, disregard and lack of respect for protective defenses or lack of patience and emotional safety
experienced in childhood.

A healthy therapeutic environment offers respect and
patience for the healing process. The therapist models
compassion and respect for the individual's creative and
healthy survival adaptation.

Whose Healing Is This Anyway?

When Jordon came for his first appointment with me,
he answered my first questions in a somewhat rote and
detached manner.

"Could you talk a little about why you've chosen to enter therapy?"

"I want to get in touch with my inner child."

"Could you say a little more about the inner child, Jordon?"

"Well, yes. My last therapist, you know where I lived before, thinks I'm co-dependent. He also told me to tell you that I've probably been sexually abused. I don't know."

"Were you sexually abused?"

"Gosh, I don't know. He says I act like a sexual abuse survivor."

"How's that?"

"Well," he started to cry. "Jane, I'm so frustrated. My old therapist said he thought I could even abuse children. I'm so scared. I feel like . . . I'm so frustrated."

"Jordon, have you been attracted to children in a sexual way?"

"No. But now I'm even afraid to be around kids. My partner has a daughter and I've been afraid to even hug her. Once when I was a little kid, I had a sexual dream about my sister. We were, you know, showing each other our bodies that day and I dreamed about her naked that night — but I never did anything. I don't know what I feel anymore. Maybe you'd better call my old therapist. He can tell you what he thinks."

"I'd really rather talk about how you think and feel about your life. So far it sounds like you're really frustrated, frightened and confused about a lot of labels and words. Maybe you could tell me why you went to your old therapist to begin with. Maybe we could start there."

"I went because I had just started a new relationship, a new job and my mother had just been diagnosed with cancer. She died about six months ago. There were so many changes in my life and my mother and I had never got along . . ."

Over the years, I have seen countless clients like Jordon come into therapy confused by labels and someone else's idea of their problems. In many ways Jordon's past therapy was a repeat of his childhood. His mother had spent her life telling him what he was and wasn't, what he felt and didn't and what he should or shouldn't do. No one had ever taken the time to listen to him and help him learn about his needs, desires and feelings, and to validate his perceptions of the world. Unfortunately, his feelings and concerns were never addressed in his early life or in his prior therapy. He grew up being controlled and overwhelmed by a narcissistic mother and continued with a therapist who considered his own agendas more important than Jordon's. He learned to survive by being passive, yet he didn't give up. He tenaciously kept seeking support for his truth.

It is extremely sad when children are forced to grow up in environments that constantly deny their perceptions and feelings. It's a travesty when that process continues in the name of healing.

A compassionate, safe and validating healing environment is one in which listening and hearing take place, where concern is shown for goals, feelings and experiences of the individual who is there to heal. When attention, concern and value are placed on the feelings and experiences of individuals, then the process of self-validation and self-respect begins to flourish.

Compassionate Healing

Countless individuals grew up in environments that were traumatic and shaming. A large percentage created resilient, adaptive coping mechanisms in order to survive their pain, such as humor, compassion, altruism, tenacity, perseverance and creativity. Unfortunately, many of the effects of shame and trauma continue into adult life and it is necessary to allow ourselves a compassionate healing process.

In order to give ourselves the same compassion that we frequently offer to others, it is important to be aware of the hurtful messages from the past, the self-hate messages we continue to give ourselves, the difference between supportive and nonsupportive healing environments and new messages that support continued growth. The following are examples of some of the steps in the process and supportive versus nonsupportive messages.

1. **Validating the effects of past traumatic and shaming environment.**

   Old environmental messages:
   - "There's nothing wrong here."
   - "What's the matter with you?"
   - "If you've been hurt, you caused it."
   - "You're bad and so are your feelings."

   Healing message — nonsupportive:

   Focus on symptoms rather than shame and trauma. Lack of validation of childhood traumas and resiliency in adaptation.
   - "What's the matter with you?"
   - "You're sick and need help."
   - "Yesterday doesn't matter. You need to focus on the problems you have today."
   - "Childhood memories are only fantasies."
   - "Your parents did the best they could. Get on with your life."
   - "Your parents are responsible for all the problems you have today."

   Healing message — supportive:

   Focus on past traumas and shaming environment. Exploration of feelings concerning early pain and humiliation. Exploration of effects of environment still carried today that may be causing difficulties, as well as the successful adaptive responses created for surviving a painful past.

- "I believe that happened to you."
- "What was your experience?"
- "Feelings are normal."
- "I have a great deal of respect for your survival. You have many strengths."
- "There are many natural effects of childhood trauma and shaming. I want to know what you experience today."
- "You are a responsible adult."

Hurtful messages to self:

- "If it happened, I must have caused it."
- "I am a victim of the pain in my past and I'll never heal."
- "I must find out what's wrong with me and correct it in a hurry in order to be worthy of others' care and compassion."
- "If they only knew, they wouldn't like me."
- "I'm making a big deal out of nothing."
- "It didn't happen. I'm just making it up."
- "I need others to validate my experiences before I can validate my own."

Healing messages to self:

- "I suffered traumas and painful shaming in my childhood for which I was not responsible."
- "I will allow myself the validation, support and time it takes to heal from the effects of a painful past."
- "As an adult, I am now responsible for my own healing as well as for other commitments I have made to myself and others."

- "In order to heal, I know I must find the support and safety in a healing environment that was unavailable to me as a child."
- "I developed many strengths to cope with pain as a child. I respect and honor those strengths today."

2. **Respect for defenses and boundaries in the process of healing.**

Old environmental message:

- "You and I are one."
- "No pain, no gain."
- "I don't have time for your problems."
- "I know what's good for you."
- "Hurry up, get it over with, whatever it is."

Healing message — nonsupportive:

- "No need for time — let's get to the core."
- "No pain, no gain."
- "Hurry up and feel."
- "We're the experts. We know what's good for you."
- "We need to break down those defenses. We need to get through them."

Healing message — supportive:

- "Healing takes time."
- "Defenses are healthy. You'll gradually let them go when it's safe."
- "You'll allow yourself to feel vulnerable when it's safe."
- "Trust takes time."
- "You'll remember when it feels safe."
- "I respect your boundaries and defenses."

Hurtful messages to self:

- "I have to remember the traumas now or the feelings don't matter."
- "I have to hurry up. I've got to get rid of these problems now."

- "Just because it doesn't feel safe doesn't mean it isn't. They're the experts, they know best."
- "Taking time is just being lazy."
- "Defenses are pathological."

Healthy messages to self:

- "I experienced a great deal of hurt as a child. I developed defenses to protect myself. Those defenses are healthy and I will let them down gradually when it's safe."
- "If I had safety and support as a child, I would have been able to heal the pain that I felt. When I have support now, I will be able to heal."
- "When I know it's safe, I will validate my own feelings."
- "Healing takes time. I can allow myself that time. I was hurried as a child. I don't need to rush myself today."

3. **Develop your own goals, not someone else's.**

Old environmental message:

- "I know what's good for you. Do it my way."
- "You don't know what happened or what you feel, I do."

Healing message — nonsupportive:

- "Let me tell you what happened to you. You can't remember but I know."
- "You don't know what you feel. Let me tell you. These are the feelings you should be feeling."

Healing messages — supportive:

- "What are your goals? What would you like to accomplish?"
- "Tell me your perception of that experience."
- "What were your feelings?"

Hurtful messages to self:

- "If they think that happened to me, it must have.

They know best."
- "Tell me what I feel. My feelings must have been wrong."
- "What are your goals for my healing? I don't know what I should want. I am always making mistakes."
- "I'm in denial. Tell me what's right."

Healthy messages to self:
- "I am the expert in my own life."
- "My feelings may change but only I can change them. I have the right to my own feelings and thoughts as an adult."
- "I may not remember my past right now but only I can remember it. Someone else can't tell me what I lived."
- "Only I can truly validate my own feelings and perceptions."

Change The Volume — Not The Channel

I have been impressed throughout my years of clinical practice with the amazing resiliency of the human spirit. My belief in the creative abilities of children to develop healthy coping mechanisms against a backdrop of tremendous pain was reinforced when I read the responses to the questions in the questionnaire and conducted recent in-depth interviews with adults who had experienced childhood trauma.

I may be an optimist when it comes to human nature but I am not an individual who wears a blindfold in light of reality. I am aware that many hundreds of individuals are not able to make healthy adaptations in the face of an abusive childhood. Many go on to repeat the abuse as adults and some of those individuals are unfortunately untreatable. Many also spend their lives in hospitals or are chronically isolated.

I am also aware that individuals like those portrayed in this book have suffered throughout their lives and these painful areas need to be addressed.

My concern is that the focus in our world, and indeed in the therapeutic community, has been skewed and out of balance for far too many years.

We have focused on symptoms of pathology and almost ignored resiliency strengths and healthy adaptive coping styles. When a Ted Bundy has committed unthinkable acts, similar to those he must have sustained in childhood, we put him in the spotlight for months and even years. Individuals stayed up at night waiting for the coverage of Bundy's death. We even heard of parents tragically, and perhaps abusively, packing a picnic buffet and taking their children on a family outing to a location where they could witness signs of his demise close up. Some announced that they did this to teach their small children a lesson in right and wrong.

We spend millions of dollars of research funds to study individuals who commit horrible crimes, yet a fraction of that money to intervene in their lives before it's too late for intervention or treatment. We also expend little time and energy protecting the victims of their crimes, many of whom are children in child care facilities.

Yet individuals who function on altruism and compassion — rescue strangers from life-threatening situations, devote their lives to helping children who were abused as they once were or who spend endless volunteer hours working with the homeless — these somehow escape our attention. Do we spend research funds to study these individuals with the possibility of perhaps intervening at

an early age with a child who has identified with the
aggressor rather than with the victim?

It would seem that this lack of balance in the application
of focus, funds, energy and attention also mimics abuses
in childhood: ignoring and neglecting the positive acts
that a child does and focusing our attention on the mistakes and problem behaviors.

The focus on pathology rather than resiliency in our
world, and indeed frequently in ourselves, reminds me
of a delightful story in *The Healing Power of Humor* by
Allen Klein:

> A very staid English lady, who had been part of one
> of the British Buddhist societies for many years, came
> one day to visit the renowned meditation teacher,
> Achaan Chaa. She asked him all kinds of complicated
> questions about meditation and the Buddhist teachings
> known as *dharma*. The teacher asked her if she had
> been doing much meditation practice itself. She said no.
> She had not had the time; she was too busy studying
> *dharma*. Achaan Chaa looked at her and replied, 'Mad-
> am, you are like the woman who keeps chickens in her
> yard and goes around picking up the chicken droppings
> instead of the eggs.'

Unfortunately, the lengthy and unbalanced focus on
pathology by the therapeutic community has frequently
resulted in the eggs being missed altogether and, as a
result, the nutrition contained within them.

The attention paid to survivors of parental alcoholism
and other childhood traumas originated to validate a reality and depathologize responses to painful childhoods.
Unfortunately, this effort eventually turned into an em-
phasis on countless symptoms of a new pathology, co-

dependency. With this new list of symptoms came, for many, a return to feelings of shame.

In order to create a compassionate healing environment, it is important to highlight healthy survival adaptation as well as the areas creating pain in a person's life. There are two sides to almost everything.

Mary's altruistic focus on foster children supports her sense of well-being and self-worth. If she becomes ill, burned out or devotes energy to foster children to the exclusion of her own children, husband or friendships, it would be important to work with Mary toward the possibility of turning the volume down on her altruistic acts in order to attain a more healthy life balance. It is not Mary's altruism or "caretaking" that is the problem. That part of her she says, "has enriched my life and helped me form a more positive concept of self." It is the volume that's the problem.

Tony is an extremely talented artist. He has attained a lot of his positive self-worth through his talent. If he finds that his focus on art is limiting his development and creating difficulties for him, then the price begins to outweigh the benefits and he might wish to address his loss of control of the volume.

Healing isn't 24 hours a day. Efforts to heal, futhermore, should not lead to pathologizing the healthy coping skills that have been creatively developed. There is nothing wrong with attaining a feeling of self-esteem from what we do or accomplish, from what we give, from our tenacity or our sense of humor. Sometimes a walk in the woods can be more beneficial on a particular day than going to a support group. Attending a comedy can sometimes be more rewarding that reading a self-help book.

Compassionate healing involves aiding individuals in making choices, learning from them and having control of the volume on behaviors and choices that affect their lives. They are the experts on the tones and frequencies of their particular channels. They deserve to reap the benefits of the programs that they have skillfully created over many years.

So Much has Changed
by M. MacKay-Brook

So much has changed
that my heart knows no limits
while I myself have them
with your help.

So much has changed
that I walk from
family room to room
and no longer find
pieces of myself
abandoned in them.

So much has changed
when I awaken each day
and find no reason to
laugh and laugh but I do
for no reason.

So much has changed
that today I no longer need you
to tell me that
so much has changed.

So much has changed that
I realize how much has

stayed the same
and thank you.

Freedom In Self-Determination

A compassionate healing environment not only aids individuals in validating painful experiences and feelings from childhood but supports the fact that they are accountable for their choices and actions today. Few things are more limiting and demeaning to an individual than participating in the creation or re-enforcement of the notion that they are victims of a painful past.

A lawyer recently asked me if I would support his client in a defense based on his abuse in childhood. He said that he had beaten his wife because his mother had physically abused him. My answer was a definite, "No!"

It is tragic that children suffered and still suffer abuses throughout their childhood. We cannot justify the contention, however, that the irresponsible choices and behaviors of adults are the responsibility of the abusive adults in their past.

Hitler was guilty of terrible crimes against individuals and an entire society, regardless of the crimes of abuse committed against him in his childhood by an abusive father. The woman who tells me that she gave up her children to foster care because her parents had deprived her of a childhood, which she has to retrieve today in order to heal, is not accepting the responsibility of her choices.

There is a huge difference in feeling empathy, rather than sympathy toward another adult individual. Sympathy implies superiority and lack of respect. If I feel responsible for the choices of the individuals with whom I work, I am attempting to take away their ego and showing them disrespect in the process. If I don't confront others with the accountability of the choices they make today but instead I join them in blaming parents for current behavior, I am showing them no more respect than they were shown in childhood. Frequently age-appropriate development was ignored. Expecting too much or too little is shaming.

Compassionate healing involves breaking free from the chains of a painful past. Attaining self-respect through accountability for choices today is part of that freedom.

A Return To Ritual And Celebration

When there have been generations of unresolved trauma in a culture due to the effects of war, poverty, oppression and abuse, the rituals or rites of passage in that culture also begin to disappear.

For instance, a soldier in the midst of war cannot go through a normal grief ritual for a friend who has just been killed in battle. Instead he must continue to fight. For him, there are no rituals or ceremonies in place. When he comes home, he is full of grief. He may drink or go through rages. A friend or grandparent may die. He is full of past grief and overloaded. He is afraid to open the door to more grief so he drinks or rages at his family instead of allowing himself to grieve. When a holiday time comes up, he is still back in the war. He can't celebrate because he is full of survival guilt. As a man full of grief, he cannot celebrate or pass on normal rituals to his family.

Countless Native Americans, Jewish Americans, African-Americans, Italian-Americans, etc., have lost the important traditions, rituals and celebrations of their cultures through acculturation and oppression. As stated so well by Peter Matthiessen in *The Circle of Life,*

> Like the primordial silence of the earth's passage
> through the universe, like the night stars lost to pollu-
> tion and artificial light, the rites that celebrate the
> mysteries of our fate are being lost. Cultures become
> homogenized as their idiosyncratic knobs and colors
> are rubbed away until, finally, nothing is left but the
> dead forms like white fossils in old rock.

The rituals and traditions of a culture are the binding force of that culture: that which gives meaning to birth, childhood, adulthood, family, death and indeed, life itself; the rites of passage from one phase of life to another, from delusion to enlightenment; and that which links and binds human beings together and connects us to the rhythm of the universe itself. Rituals and traditions are the frameworks around which we celebrate the birth of a child, the passage from childhood to adulthood, the commitment to a life partner, grief over a loss or a death, the way we celebrate important mileposts and passages in our lives, as well as the meaning we have given to life itself.

A majority of the individuals I have worked with over the years did not feel welcomed into their families or community. Many had never had a celebration of their birth. Yet, at one time there were rituals in every culture to celebrate a new life and to welcome that child into the community. Ceremonies and rituals were extremely different from culture to culture but each, according to Marquez and Matthiessen, said essentially the same thing: Welcome. You are one of us. With the help of God — or Christ — or Allah or the Crocodile Spirit of the Septik River — we will do our best to protect and nurture you. With these words, spoken in vast cities and tiny villages, in a thousand different languages, we begin our voyage on the circle of life.

Part of a compassionate healing process is to revitalize old rituals or begin new ones, new traditions and celebrations for ourselves, our families and communities.

Mary, mentioned earlier, lovingly prepared a basket for each foster child who came into her home, a ritual of welcome. Many have begun traditional birthday celebrations, new rituals around loss and grief, celebrations of seasons, religious holidays, mileposts, traditional celebrations to mark their children passing from childhood to adolescence, commitment rituals or celebrations of midlife rather than acting out crisis.

Bea Shawanda, a Native American woman of the Odawa-Pottowahomi band, offered me a gift of new celebration when she shared with me the meaning of menopause in her language: "birth of woman." It was a time in life, according to the old ones, for celebration, not depression or crisis. It was the time in a woman's life when she became a woman in her own right, rather than as a child, partner or mother.

When individuals have completed their therapy work with me, I ask them to plan the final session with a celebration or ritual that would, for them, give meaning to this particular passage. I have been continually impressed by the thought, creativity, symbolism, emotion and meaning they have brought to this task and the rituals and ceremonies created. Over the years there have not been two identical closing sessions. Each has been as unique as the individual and the particular griefwork. Many have incorporated the metaphors and rituals used in that final session into other rites of passage in their lives in the future.

Linda Weltner, in her book, *No Place Like Home*, speaks to the meaning of celebration and ritual as she contemplates the feelings she experienced while planning her daughter's birthday party.

My reward came from the love I felt when picking out the balloons and candles. I know these are gestures I do because of the feelings they engender in me. They give expression to the artist within me, not on canvas, but in the trivial, daily acts of existence. I embroider, I draw, I sculpt in small acts designed to make my life and my surroundings a more fitting reflection of myself.

Reach Out And Touch Somebody's Hand

Last year, during a long layover in O'Hare airport, I had two experiences that profoundly affected me. The first was a chance meeting with a wonderful little African-American boy and his grandmother. They had been stuck in the airport for almost 24 hours. The little boy was very active despite his obvious weariness and the grandmother, Elizabeth, was too tired for words. I offered to help her with Joseph so she could get some rest. She looked at me suspiciously at first and asked why. I said, "Because you're tired, I've had some rest and I've had the experience of raising four boys as active as Joseph. Besides," I said laughing, "I'm younger than you are." As it turned out, we helped each other throughout the grueling wait of many more hours and false departures in the blizzard conditions. Being with each other, spelling each other and sharing company and care made the wait much easier for all of us.

The next day I was stranded again. I ran to catch my plane but missed it. In the attempt, I fell down and scraped my leg. It was bleeding and I was toting two heavy carryons. When I saw an elderly lady at my gate, I asked her if she could watch my bags for just a minute until I could wash and bandage my leg. She looked at me angrily. I explained that the restroom was a distance. She said abruptly, "Lady, your problems have nothing to do with me. Take care of your own problems!" Fortunately, a gentleman in a nearby seat heard the conversation and offered any assistance he could give me.

One of the tragedies of living in a culture and world that has denied child abuse, neglect and the effects of unresolved trauma, is the breakdown of families and communities. Isolation is a byproduct of a community in pain. When we find ourselves saying, *That's his problem, not mine* — or *Look out for Number One* — we are essentially saying that we hurt too much and feel too powerless to risk connecting again with a world that has deeply injured us.

To say that this isolation is inevitable in the future, that it is the destiny of the human race or the true wish of individuals is, in my opinion, incorrect. I believe that compassion and reaching out are in the inherent nature of the healthy human being. We are a communal people, not meant to live in isolation. When we are given models of compassion for others, we pass on that compassion.

Morton Hunt spoke to this modeling process in his book, *The Compassionate Beast.*

> More people will put money in a Salvation Army kettle, a blind beggar's cup and the like if they have just seen someone else do so than if they haven't. Other experiments, employing news stories or broadcasts of altruistic acts, have likewise shown that there is a kind of contagion of benevolent behavior; people who have just heard of an altruistic act are more inclined to respond to someone in need than people who have not. Many of us can attest to that: We read of the outpouring of donations by other people to victims of floods, famine or earthquake and reach for our pen and checkbook.

I have witnessed the effect of modeling on my own children as well as on their friends at times. One of the rituals that I encouraged with my children was putting something under the "Giving Tree" during the Christmas season in the city in which we lived. The Giving Tree is usually a tree in a central location that contains the names and wishes of a child whose family is having a difficult time financially during the holiday season. You take a paper ball off the tree that has the child's name and age on one side and a requested gift on the other.

One year when the boys were still in grade school, our family and one of their friends went out for our traditional cocoa and trip to the Giving Tree. We had just taken the names when I saw three young and obviously wealthy pre-adolescent boys on the other side of the tree taking names off and laughing as they ripped the paper balls to pieces. I couldn't believe it. I walked around and confronted them.

"What are you doing?"

One laughed and responded, "It's none of your business."

Two of my sons, Jason and Damien came around the tree. "Don't you know these are names of children who can't afford a Christmas?" they asked, almost in unison, shocked at the behavior of the older boys.

"Yeah, so what?"

"Do you have any idea what it would feel like to be one of these children and wake up on Christmas morning?" I asked.

I realized by this time that my oldest and youngest sons, Shawn and Forrest, had gone to fetch a nearby security guard. The guard came almost immediately and took the boys off with him.

Five years later, my son Damien and the same friend who was with us that day, were at the same mall and witnessed two young adolescents laughing and taking the tags off the tree. They intervened, responding the same way I had five years before.

Unfortunately, the Giving Tree in that wealthy mall is now a thing of the past. Not only were the names taken off year after year but the donated presents kept disappearing as well.

Rebuilding A Sense Of Community

One of the promises that I made to myself many years ago was that I'd never watch child abuse around me again without intervening. I make this statement whenever I talk to a group and the response I get is genuine interest and applause followed by, "I want to do that, too. I just have never known how. Can you give me some examples?"

One of the things that I learned growing up from my Native American elder was, "*The honor of one is the honor of all and the pain of one is the pain of all.*" Unfortunately, that type of philosophy is seen by many today as co-dependency. Human beings are communal. We count on each other — not only on ourselves — for survival. Like drops of water in a clear pond, we are all connected. A ripple in the pond spreads and creates other ripples.

Bea Shawanda, of the Odawa-Pottowahomi band in Canada and a national trainer with the National Association of Treatment Directors, told me two stories recently that reflected the importance of community healing. Bea was asked to go into a community where there had been an epidemic of adolescent suicides. One of the things she saw that was inspiring in the face of such pain was the organization of parents that occurred prior to her arrival. Parents of adolescents lost to suicide had formed an intervention team. When they heard of an attempted suicide or a possible suicide, they went as a group to the family of the adolescent and intervened with the entire family, sometimes staying up all night. The interventions, the show of care and support from individuals so obviously hurting, re-enforced the sharing of pain and the rebuilding of a community rather than self-destruction. When asked about their decision to form the team, they replied that the healing of others' pain assisted in their own healing process.

At one point, Bea returned to her own community to reopen an addiction treatment center. As in the Indian way, a feast was planned for the celebration of the opening and a large supply of turkeys was purchased.

In the process of becoming reacquainted with her community after a long absence, Bea noticed that there was a woman, a local bootlegger and alcoholic, who had been isolated from the community. The day before the feast, Bea went to the woman's house carrying a turkey. She said that the woman was clearly surprised to see her there. Bea said, "I really need your help. We're having a feast, as you may know, at the center and we have all these turkeys. You have a big family and I've heard you're a good cook. I wondered if you could help us out. We really need your help with this." The woman, still surprised, said she'd be glad to help.

As Bea was leaving, she said, "We'd really like you to come to the center for the feast tomorrow night to help us celebrate. If you can't make it, then I'll pick up the turkey before the feast but we'd really like you to be there." To Bea's surprise, the woman came to the feast, turkey in hand. She was welcomed back into the community. She now comes to the center all the time and celebrates her sobriety.

I believe it is the wish of individuals to be a part of a community and a world culture. When given the opportunity, children and adults alike show a need to help and belong.

A number of weeks ago, I received a baby announcement from a couple who were healing from abusive backgrounds. There was a mimeographed letter enclosed which once again re-enforced my belief in the compassion of human beings.

"We are privileged to be able to bring our new son up in a household in which his material needs can be more than adequately met. We hope you will consider this occasion an opportunity to help ensure that all children receive the sustenance and protection they deserve. While we would be delighted with personal gifts (drawings, songs, poems) to celebrate our child's birth, we would also be honored if you would consider making a donation to Sanctuary for Families, The Children's Defense Fund or the Center for Prevention of Sexual and Domestic Violence in support of their work on behalf of children and families."

As reported in Sylvia Ann Hewlett's work, *When the Bough Breaks,* child abuse in the United States "has quadrupled since 1975 . . . Twenty percent of the nation's children are being raised in poverty."

Many of the resilient adults in my study suffered the painful childhood effects of poverty, cultural oppression, physical and sexual abuse, war, sibling death, parental alcoholism, parental suicide, unresolved loss and emotional abuse. Forty percent of the 200 respondents said their greatest childhood fear was abandonment and another 22 percent feared violence or being killed.

The majority of the adults in my survey listed a sense of humor, compassion, altruism, tenacity, perseverance and creativity as their saving graces in childhood as well as the qualities that they are still using and are proud of today.

Seventy-five percent of those responding to the questionnaire said that they received the most comfort in their childhoods from involvement with animals, nature or reading books. Although only 36 out of 200 stated that they received the most comfort from people, all of the resilient adults that I interviewed in depth could point to at least one adult who offered them care, modeling and hope during painful childhood years. The contact with that adult who reached out may have been minimal — a teacher, neighbor or distant relative — but it was enough, however, to add meaning and hope to a painful life.

Rebuilding a compassionate community and world not only insures our future growth as individuals but the growth and resiliency of our greatest future resource, our children.

Compassionate healing involves validating the pain in our past and recognizing that the shame and trauma of painful childhood environments was not a fantasy or our fault; focusing on defining current problem areas in our lives and healing without labeling ourselves in the process; allowing ourselves time and safety in healing; maintaining a balance in our lives as we heal the wounds of a painful past; remaining responsible for our choices today; focusing on the multitude of events and influences that have shaped our lives; celebrating our strengths and resiliency; learning and modeling healthy values, traditions and rituals; and sharing our strengths and lessons compassionately and respectfully with others as we help rebuild families and communities based on mutual support for our continued growth and the healthy development of our children.

I recently saw a poster that summed up the knowledge that can be gained as a result of compassionate healing:

We have not inherited the earth
From our fathers
We are borrowing it
From our children.

A Native American saying of
unknown origin and author

Questionnaire

The following questionnaire was developed to pursue my study of resiliency characteristics in children of traumatic background. Two hundred responses were collected, including 50 men and 150 women with a wide range of ages and occupations. The majority came from families, school systems or communities that were experienced as shaming, traumatic or abusive. Seven in-depth interviews on the subjective impressions of survival adaptation in children were also conducted.

Completing the questionnaire slowly and thoughtfully can be extremely valuable. You will see where you have been, how you coped, how far you have come and what you have learned.

You may check more than one answer when that is appropriate. If you need more space, continue on back of sheet. (Use question number.)

1. Current age _____

2. Male _____ Female _____

3. How many siblings in your family of origin? _____

4. You were: Oldest child _____ Middle child _____
   Youngest child _____

5. Who took care of whom in the family? _____
   (Example: Mother took care of Dad — my sister took
   care of the siblings.)

6. How would you describe the atmosphere of your
   family?
   Co-operative _____ Competitive _____
   Antagonistic _____ Anxious _____
   Violent _____ Cold _____ Repressed _____
   Every one for him/herself _____ Noisy _____
   Chaotic _____ Inconsistent _____ Distant _____
   Sarcastic _____ Confusing _____ Fun-loving _____
   Shaming _____ Silent _____ Abusive _____
   Creative _____
   Other (specify) _____

7. How would you describe your parents' relationship?
   _____
   _____

8. What made a person valuable in the family?
   _____
   _____

9. Who did the punishing? _____
   Who did the rewarding? _____

10. What was your family's status in the community?
    Respected _____ Looked down on _____
    Well known _____ Other _____

11. What was the neighborhood like where you grew up?
    Rural _____ City _____ Suburban _____
    Other (specify) _____

12. What was your class level?
    Upper _____ Middle _____ Lower _____

13. What is your cultural-ethnic background? _____

14. What kind of school did you attend?
    Public _____ Private _____

15. To whom did you feel valuable in school?
    Peers _____ Teachers _____
    The community as a whole _____

16. (a) Identify the following traumas that affected your
    parents' lives. (Put a "P" next to the trauma listed.)
    (b) Identify the following traumas that affected your
    life directly. (Put an "S" next to the trauma listed.)

Alcoholism	Religious fanaticism
Substance abuse	Cult
Poverty	Death of a sibling
Cultural self-hate	Death of a parent
Sexual abuse (overt)	Adoption
Sexual abuse (covert)	Divorce
Violence (overt)	Physical handicaps
Violence (covert)	Physical illness
Immigration	War survivor
Depression	Holocaust survivorship
Mental illness	Concentration camp survivor

Suicide   Boarding schools
Abandonment   Unknown
Loss of financial security   Other (specify) _____
Affluence   _____

17. When I was sad or upset, I turned to:
    A parent _____ A sibling _____ A peer _____
    A teacher _____ A grandparent _____
    A neighbor _____ Family friend _____
    Member of my religious faith _____
    Kept to myself _____ The family pet _____
    A toy or object _____ Other _____

18. Before 13, I felt the most comfort from involvement
    with:
    People _____ Animals _____ Nature _____
    God _____ Art _____ Reading _____
    Dance _____ Music _____ Writing _____
    Athletics _____ Other _____

19. My favorite childhood story or fairy tale was _____
    _____

20. Who or what I most identified with in the childhood
    story or fairy tale was _____

21. When I was a child, I most wanted to grow up and be
    like _____
    Why? (person you knew or knew through books, etc.)
    _____

22. My childhood ambition was _____
    _____

23. My greatest childhood fear was _____
    _____

24. My saving grace in childhood was my _____
    (personal characteristic — example: artistic ability,
    sense of humor, sensitivity, etc.)

25. Did you have fantasy parents? _____ What were
    they like? (Attributes you gave one or more parents
    that you know they did not have.) _____

26. The survival skill that I am most proud of today is
    _____

27. The survival skills that I still use today are _____
    _____

28. My current profession is _____

29. If I had time and money I would contribute to _____
    _____

30. An important area that you have forgotten that I
    would like to comment on is _____
    _____
    _____
    _____

Bibliography

Aberbach, David. **Loss and Separation in Bialik and Wordsworth.** Prooftexts. Baltimore: Johns Hopkins University Press, 1982. Vol. 2.

Aberbach, David. **At the Handles of the Lock.** Oxford: Oxford University Press, 1982.

Bettelheim, Bruno. **The Meaning and Importance of Fairy Tales.** New York: Vintage Books, 1977.

Bettelheim, Bruno. **Surviving and Other Essays.** New York: Vintage Books, 1980.

Bleuler, M. "The Offspring of Schizophrenics." *Schizophrenia Bulletin.* 1974, 8: 93-107.

Boone, J. Allen. **The Language of Silence.** New York: Harper and Row Publishers, 1970.

Branden, Nathaniel. **Honoring The Self: The Psychology of Confidence and Respect.** New York: Bantam Books, 1983.

Branden, Nathaniel. **Honoring The Self: Personal Integrity and The Heroic Potentials of Human Nature.** Los Angeles: Jeremy Tarcher, Inc., 1983.

Bresler, David and Turbo, Richard. **Free Yourself From Pain.** New York: Simon and Schuster, 1979.

Chapman, Antony and Fout, Hugh (eds.). **Humor and Laughter: Theory, Research and Applications.** London: Wiley and Sons, 1976.

Chopra, Deepak. **Unconditional Life: Mastering the Forces that Shape Personal Reality.** New York: Bantam Books, 1991.

Clarke, Jean I. **Self-Esteem: A Family Affair.** San Francisco: Harper and Row, 1978.

Coffee, Gerald. **Beyond Survival: A POW's Inspiring Lesson in Living.** New York: Berkley Books, 1990.

Cohen, David (ed.). **The Circle of Life: Rituals From the Human Family Album.** San Francisco: Harper Collins, 1991.

Cornell, Joseph. **Listening to Nature: How to Deepen Your Awareness of Nature.** Nevada City, CA: Dawn Publications, 1987.

Cousins, Norman. **Anatomy of an Illness.** New York: W.W. Norton and Company, 1979.

Diamond, John. **Your Body Doesn't Lie.** New York: Warner, 1979.

Dillon, Kathleen and Tutten, Mary. "Psychological Factors, Immunocompetence and Health of Breast-Feeding." *Journal of Genetic Psychology.* 1989, 150: 155-162.

Dyer, Wayne. **The Sky's the Limit.** New York: Pocket Books, 1980.

Engel, Lewis and Ferguson, Tom. **Imaginary Crimes: Why We Punish Ourselves and How to Stop.** Boston: Houghton Mifflin Company, 1990.

Erikson, Erik H. **Gandhi's Truth: On the Origins of Militant Nonviolence.** New York: W.W. Norton and Company, 1969.

Fahy, Mary. **The Tree That Survived the Winter.** Mahwah, NJ: Paulist Press, 1989.

Fay, Allen. **Making Things Better by Making Them Worse.** New York: Hawthorn Books, 1978.

Fisher, Seymour and Fisher, Rhoda. **Pretend the World is Funny and Forever.** Hillsdale, NJ: L. Eribaum, 1981.

Flach, Frederic. **Resilience: Discovering a New Strength at Times of Stress.** New York: Fawcett Columbine, 1988.

Frankl, Viktor. **The Unheard Cry for Meaning: Psychotherapy and Humanism.** New York: Simon and Schuster, Inc., 1978.

Frankl, Viktor. **Man's Search for Meaning (rev. ed.).** New York: Pocket Books, 1984.

Freud, Sigmund. "Wit and Its Relation to the Unconscious." Quoted in Seldes, George. (ed.) **The Great Thoughts.** New York: Ballantine Books, 1985. pp. 143-144.

Frey, William and Langseth, Muriel. **Crying: The Mystery of Tears.** New York: Harper and Row, 1985.

Frost, Robert. **The Road Not Taken: A Selection of Robert Frost's Poems.** New York: Henry Holt and Company, 1971.

Fry, William F. Jr. and Allen, Melanie. **Make 'em Laugh: Life Studies of Comedy Writers.** Palo Alto, CA: Science and Behavior Books, 1975.

Fry, William F., Jr. and Salameh, Waleed A. (eds.). **Handbook of Humor and Psychotherapy.** Sarasota, Florida: Professional Resource Exhange, 1986.

Gendler, J. Ruth. **The Book of Qualities.** New York: Harper and Row, 1988.

Ghiselin, Brewster (ed.). **The Creative Process: A Symposium.** New York: Penguin Books, 1952.

Glaser, Frederick B. "The Case of Franz Kafka." *The Psychoanalytic Review.* 1964, 51: 99-121.

Grinker, R. "On Identification." *International Journal of Psychoanalysis.* 1957, 38: 379-390.

Grolnick, Simon A. "Emily Dickinson: The Interweaving of Poetry and Personality." *The Psychoanalytic Review.* 1990, 77: 111-131.

Gruner, Charles. **Understanding Laughter: The Workings of Wit and Humor.** Chicago: Nelson-Hall, 1978.

Guerney, Louise F. "A Survey of Self-Supports and Social Supports of Self-Care Children." *Elementary School Guidance and Counseling.* 1991, 25: 243-254.

Hewlett, Sylvia. **When the Bough Breaks: The Cost of Neglecting Our Children.** New York: Basic Books, 1991.

Hunt, Morton. **The Compassionate Beast: The Scientific Inquiry into Human Altruism.** New York: Doubleday, 1990.

James, Muriel and James, John. **Passion for Life: Psychology and the Human Spirit.** New York: Dutton, 1991.

Katz, Stan and Liv, Aimee. **The Codependency Conspiracy: How to Break the Recovery Habit and Take Charge of Your Life.** New York: Warner Books, 1991.

Kaufman, Lois, L. (ed.). **Time for Reflection.** White Plains, NY: Peter Pauper Press, 1991.

Klein, Allen. **The Healing Power of Humor.** Los Angeles: Jeremy P. Tarcher, Inc., 1990.

Kohn, Alfie. **The Brighter Side of Human Nature: Altruism and Empathy in Everyday Life.** New York: Basic Books, 1990.

Konner, Melvin. **Why the Reckless Survive and Other Secrets of Human Nature.** New York: Viking, 1990.

Lane, Margaret. **The Tale of Beatrix Potter.** London: Warne, 1970.

Lasch, Christopher. **The Culture of Narcissism: American Life in an Age of Diminishing Expectations.** New York: W.W. Norton and Company, 1979.

Lerner, Michael. **Surplus Powerlessness: The Psychodynamics of Everyday Life . . . and the Psychology of the Individual and Social Transformations.** Oakland, CA: Institute for Labor and Mental Health, 1986.

Lifton, Robert J. **The Life of the Self: Toward a New Psychology.** New York: Basic Books, 1983.

Linscott, Robert (ed.). **Selected Poems and Letters of Emily Dickinson.** New York: Anchor Books, Doubleday, 1959.

Lyshak, Frances, Bassin, Donna and Robbins, Arthur. "The Creative Act as a Means of Overcoming Resistance in Treatment." *The Psychoanalytic Review.* 1981, 68: 395-407.

Martin, Rod. "Humor and the Mastery of Living: Using Humor to Cope With the Daily Stresses of Growing Up." *Journal of Children in Contemporary Society.* 1988, 20: 135-154.

Maslach, Christina. **Burnout — The Cost of Caring.** New York: Prentice Hall Press, 1982.

May, Rollo. **The Courage to Create.** New York: Bantam Books, 1975.

May, Rollo. **My Quest for Beauty.** Dallas, Texas: Saybrook Publishing Company, 1985.

May, Rollo. **The Cry for Myth.** New York: W.W. Norton and Company, 1991.

Mayeroff, Milton. **On Caring.** New York: Harper and Row, 1971.

Mazlish, Bruce. **The Leader, The Led And The Psyche.** Hanover, New Hampshire: University Press of New England, 1990.

McGhee, Paul E. **Humor: Origins and Development.** San Francisco, CA: W.H. Freeman and Company, 1979.

McWilliams, Nancy. "The Psychology of the Altruist." *Psychoanalytic Psychology.* 1984, 1: 193-213.

Meacham, Andrew. "Louie Anderson: A Comedian Who's Serious About Recovery." *Changes.* Jan. Feb. 1990.

Middelton-Moz, Jane and Dwinell, Lorie. **After the Tears: Reclaiming the Personal Losses of Childhood.** Pompano Beach, FL: Health Communications, 1986.

Middelton-Moz, Jane. **Children of Trauma: Rediscovering Your Discarded Self.** Deerfield Beach, FL: Health Communications, 1989.

Middelton-Moz, Jane. **Shame and Guilt: Masters of Disguise.** Deerfield Beach, FL: Health Communications, 1990.

Miller, Alice. **For Your Own Good: Hidden Cruelty in Child-Rearing and the Roots of Violence.** New York: Farrar, Straus, Giroux, 1985.

Miller, Alice. **The Untouched Key: Tracing Childhood Trauma in Creativity and Destructiveness.** New York: Doubleday, 1990.

Miller, Alice. **Breaking Down the Wall of Silence: The Liberating Experience of Facing Painful Truth.** New York: Dutton, 1991.

Millman, Dan. **Secret of the Peaceful Warrior: A Story of Courage and Love.** Tiburon, CA: Starseed Press, 1991.

O'Connell, Walter E. "Resignation, Humor and Wit." *The Psychoanalytic Review,* 1964, 51:49-56.

Paulus, Trina. **Hope For the Flowers.** New York: Paulist Press, 1972.

Peacock, Mary. "The Importance of Crying." *Ms.* June, 1980: 45-55.

Peele, Stanton. **Diseasing of America: Addiction Treatment Out of Control.** Boston: Houghton Mifflin Co., 1989.

Rappaport, Ernst A. "From the Keystone of Comedy to the Last of the Clowns." *The Psychoanalytic Review.* 1972, 59:333-346.

Rhodes, Richard. **A Hole in the World: An American Boyhood.** New York: Simon and Schuster, 1990.

Rubin, Theodore. **Compassion and Self-Hate: An Alternative to Despair.** New York: Collier Books, 1975.

Sands, Steven. "The Use of Humor in Psychotherapy." *The Psychoanalytic Review.* 1984, 71:441-460.

Sanford, Linda, T. **Strong at the Broken Places: Overcoming the Trauma of Childhood Abuse.** New York: Random House, 1990.

Sanville, Jean. "Creativity and the Constructing of the Self." *The Psychoanalytic Review,* 1987, 74:263-279.

Seligman, Martin. **Helplessness: On Depression, Development and Death.** New York: W.H. Freeman and Co., 1975.

Sheehy, Gail. **Pathfinders.** New York: Bantam Books, 1981.

Siegel, Bernie S. **Love, Medicine & Miracles.** New York: Harper and Row, 1986.

Simon, Richard K., "Freud's Concept of Comedy and Suffering." *The Psychoanalytic Review.* 1977, 64:391-407.

Simonton, O. Carl, Simonton, Stephanie-Matthews and Creighton, James. **Getting Well Again.** Los Angeles: J.P. Tarcher, 1978.

Smith, Charles. **From Wonder to Wisdom: Using Stories to Help Children Grow.** New York: Penguin Books, 1989.

Spitz, Ellen H. "The Artistic Image and the Inward Gaze: Toward a Merging of Perspectives." *The Psychoanalytic Review.* 1988, 75:111-128.

Storr, Anthony. **Solitude: A Return to the Self.** New York: The Free Press, Macmillan, 1988.

Storr, Anthony. **Churchill's Black Dog, Kafka's Mice and Other Phenomena of the Human Mind.** New York: Ballantine Books, 1990.

Terr, Lenore. "Childhood Trauma and the Creative Product: A Look at the Early Lives and Later Works of Poe, Wharton, Magritte, Hitchcock, and Bergmann." Presentation at the Annual Meeting, American Academy of Child and Adolescent Psychiatry. October 17, 1986, Los Angeles, CA.

Terr, Lenore. **Too Scared to Cry: Psychic Trauma in Childhood.** New York: Harper and Row, 1990.

Vaillant, George E. **Adaption to Life.** Boston: Little Brown and Co., 1977.

Viorst, Judith. **Necessary Losses.** New York: Fawcett Gold Medal Book, Ballantine Books, 1986.

Vorhaus, Pauline G. "The Development of Optimism During Therapy." *The Psychoanalytic Review.* 1977, 64:455-459.

Weltner, Linda. **No Place Like Home: Rooms and Reflections from One Family's Life.** New York: Arbor House, W. Morrow, 1988.

Werner, Emmy and Smith, Ruth. **Vulnerable But Invincible: A Longitudinal Study of Resilient Children and Youth.** New York: Adams, Bannister, Cox, 1989.

Wood, Nancy. **Many Winters.** New York: Doubleday and Co., 1974.